# A TALE OF TWO LEADERS

## More Growth, Bigger Freedom, Greater Impact

## Chad Missildine

The Stephen Group

# CONTENTS

# INTRODUCTION

*You can have everything in life you want if you*
*help enough people get what they want.*

Zig Ziglar

I f you are an entrepreneur, organizational leader, business leader, or simply someone who wants to grow, I'm glad you decided to read or listen to this book.

I'm a cut to the chase kind of guy so let me ask you a cut to the chase kind of question: What is it that you really want? Here are three things almost every leader I know wants. I would guess that you are likely looking for these three things too.

## 1. You want to grow and scale both your revenue and your team.

If you are like most of the leaders we work with, you want to grow and scale your revenue and team. Growth is a fundamental aspect of any organization or business. Growing is why we are in business, and growing is what keeps us in business.

If we aren't growing, we are dying. If we aren't stewarding our financial capital, we will struggle. If we aren't adding value to our customers and stakeholders, our businesses won't survive. I've yet to meet someone that has said, "No, I think I'd like to just exist with my organization and float along until it someday withers and goes away." No one says that!

**2. You want more time, margin, and freedom for what you love.**

I imagine if you are anything at all like me, you also want more precious time and margin for your family, passions, or new ventures. But you also want to spend less time working and less time in the weeds. You want to spend less time on the things that drain the life out of you.

I have yet to meet a leader that said, "No, I love working long hours, outside my passions and giftings, and away from the people and things I care about." Nobody says that, for sure!

We all want more time with the people we love. You may love spending time with friends you care about, or you have a family you are trying to raise, and you don't want to miss out on precious time and memories.

You likely want more time to pursue your passions. You might even be thinking or dreaming about new opportunities in the marketplace or new product lines. Maybe you are thinking about a new form of passive or active income like property ownership or a spin-off company. These are all great things to want. It is your life.

**3. You want to have a more significant impact through your efforts.**

Not only do you want to grow your business and create margin for the things you love, but you likely want your business to be a catalyst for good. You want to help the people you lead, the communities you serve, and the marketplace as a whole. Deep down inside, you were not born to sell widgets, punch a clock or make a quick buck.

> *You are not here by accident. You are on this earth to live on purpose and to make a difference in the world.*

I've never met anyone who didn't want to make the world a little bit better.

These three wants, in my humble experience, sum up what most leaders want. Most leaders want to grow their business and team, have more time and freedom for what they love, and make their unique mark in the world. Who wouldn't want those three things?

**Here is the problem.**

Like an elusive unicorn, most of the leaders I've known over the last twenty years don't have all three. I know how frustrating this can be. I get it. I've owned, led, and worked with many organizations. I know how frustrating and difficult it can be to grow a team of people and scale up revenue.

It is not easy to find margin along the way. There are too many leaders sacrificing their freedom, family or health to win in their business. I've been there. It is devastating to see well-intended leaders win in their work, but in the end, lose their soul, their family, or their health as a result.

And having a more significant impact in the world? This aspiration can seem unreachable. It is tough enough to grow revenue and have a life too, much less impact people and make a unique mark on the world. Unfortunately, most don't get to this point, settling for profit over purpose. While others have a small impact in the world but can't sustain the revenue and growth to support their cause and in the end, don't last.

I've wrestled with these same desires for the last two decades. We've worked toward these goals in our own organizations. I have mentored and coached over a thousand leaders with these similar dreams, desires, and struggles.

Over time, I began to notice themes and similarities in what works for leaders. I've also discovered what types of efforts seem to fall short.

I've had a few dozen big "aha" moments over the years. I've made plenty of mistakes along the way. But we have seen quite a few results. Our little companies have doubled and tripled in growth using the principles in this book. And today, I have more margin than ever before for the people and things I care about the most.

Now, I get to pursue my deepest passion in life, impacting the world by investing in leaders **like you**.

Our clients are growing more than ever before too, some by 20%, 50% or even 200% or more. Many are growing their businesses and teams. They are finding more margin and freedom for the people and passions they love the most. Many are even working fewer hours, taking more vacations, and having more fun along the way.

Some are living out a more profound sense of purpose and having the impact they want to have in their world. There is no better feeling out there! You will hear actual stories from these leaders in this book.

**Why most leaders fail.**

So why do so many leaders fail to grow their business and team? Why are there so many people trapped in their work? Why do so many lack freedom or precious margin in their lives? Why do so many people never step into their passions and purpose and fail to impact the world in their unique way?

I've been asking these questions for years. I'll be sharing my thoughts in the stories to come. For now, here are a few reasons why most leaders fail and never get what they want in their leadership and life.

There are many reasons for this failure, all centered around the topic of leadership. And there are a lot of great leadership resources out there. We all know, everything rises and falls on leadership. Many of those books point to a wide variety of insightful leadership topics.

In this book, we'll dig into the most common mistakes leaders make around these three specific issues: scaling a business and its teams, finding or keeping some sense of freedom or margin and having an impact in the world.

## Mistake 1: Unhealthy leaders.

*Unhealthy leaders create unhealthy followers.*

Most leaders are accidental in their development. As a result, many are not at a healthy place in life or work.

In contrast, healthy and growing teams only come from healthy and growing leaders. In the coming chapters, you'll hear stories of two leaders who are unhealthy in both their lives and leadership.

You will listen to their struggles, pain, and challenges in their lives, families, and teams. You'll see the intentional steps these leaders take to work on themselves. As they get healthier, you'll watch them shift their focus off of themselves and onto the people they lead and the customers and clients they are impacting.

## Mistake 2: No plan to develop people.

Another big mistake many leaders make? Most leaders take the wrong approach to developing their people, or worse, no approach at all. I've been guilty of it. Many of us have found and hired the next big all-star employee with high hopes and good intentions.

*Most teams bring on top talent, then*
*watch them wither away at their laptop*
*without the right level of support.*

I can't tell you how many leaders I have coached that want to have the right people. They know they need great people to sustain growth, reach customers, and scale. But all too often, most of these leaders don't have a plan to develop, grow and keep people for the long term.

I call this "The Good Luck" approach, and again, I have been guilty of this mistake in the past. The Good Luck approach is when a well-intended leader hires good people.

Then the leader says something like, "Here is your laptop and coffee mug. Oh, here is my number if you need anything. Better yet, just send me an email. Wow, I hope you make it longer than the last person. Okay, good luck."

Why do leaders use The Good Luck approach? Well, many reasons. Most are too busy; many are too distracted or are simply unaware.

Unfortunately, most technical leaders teach technical skills, and that is it. They do nothing to develop their employees' emotional intelligence or leadership skills. These are skills that can set their team apart from their competition over time.

These entrepreneurs and organizational leaders fail to develop and raise up future leaders to lead at a higher level. As a result, their teams fail to stay relevant in an ever-changing marketplace. Instead of high-performing, agile teams, these leaders have groups of underdeveloped individuals. Here is a stat on teams that may surprise you.

*In our experience and research, we have found that most teams function at around 58% of their potential.*

Think about that for a minute. That means most leaders and teams are reaching about half of their capacity. Why?

*One big reason teams don't reach their potential: A lack of a plan.*

If you lack a plan for developing people, and I bet you likely do, you are in the right place. In the pages to follow, we'll help you with a few key things. We'll show you how to assess where your leaders and teams are today, and we'll give you a simple way to measure their success and growth tomorrow.

We'll also show you a simple plan to help you and your team grow over time. We'll even help you raise up other leaders to multiply your leadership and impact for years to come.

**Mistake 3: Summed up in one word. People.**

In a few words: Not having the right people. I can't tell you how many times I have heard the following, yet ever familiar phrase, "I just can't find good help these days." If I had a crisp 100 dollar bill every time I heard that phrase from leaders, let's say Ben Franklin and I would be good buds.

Missing the right people is one of the most significant limitations for growth among leaders and teams. Nothing seems more frustrating to leaders than working with people. Have you worked with, talked with, or dealt with people lately? We can be a frustrating bunch!

A huge reason many leaders struggle scaling revenue and scaling a team? Most don't know how to find, hire and empower the right people. It is very tough to find, motivate and keep committed people that share your values.

What are the results of having the wrong people around you on a team?

Instead of alignment, many experience drama. Instead of buy-in and passion, most leaders deal with apathy or resistance from their team.

Instead of clarity, many leaders deal with miscommunication. Instead of high-performing teams, most have low or average performing groups of people.

In this book, you'll discover a fresh approach to attracting, hiring, and onboarding the right people. You'll hear stories from actual leaders using a specific process to set their teams up for success. You'll see a team with low engagement rates and low performance. You'll watch them skyrocket to high engagement and high performance.

**Mistake 4: Do everything.**

On the opposite side of the spectrum is another common mistake we see leaders make: They try to do everything. Some leaders we meet are simply doing too much to try to develop people. Yet, they do so without any consistency, follow-through, or action plan. I call this "The Blender Approach."

The Blender Approach is when leaders take every "leadership" ingredient under the sun. Then, they throw it into a blender with no strategy to keep everyone on their team moving in the same direction. They do something different every week or month with their teams.

I know many leaders that do so many things, living out The Blender Approach. I used to be guilty of dumping countless resources on past teams. I would share so much, there was no way anyone would ever be able to put into practice what they were learning.

Many entrepreneurs and executives I know do this often. These well-intended leaders will introduce a new topic, book, podcast, idea of the month, horoscope, or speaker each month or week. You get the idea. Lots of things are happening. It feels like there is momentum.

But in the end, confusion wins the day. Why? Because every new idea takes you in a new direction. Instead of helping drive revenue and grow people, this approach distracts everyone. It doesn't help in the end.

The Blender Approach is like someone having curable cancer. But instead of a targeted treatment, the doctor gives a different painkiller each week. The patient receives the illusion of a cure but only finds short-term relief.

When the leader does something so different every month, people know they never have to follow through on anything. Why? They know it will be something new next month and likely forgotten anyway. Talk about a waste of time and resources! Please don't make this mistake. It is not healthy or sustainable.

In the coming chapters, you'll hear from two different leaders, Ben and Hannah. Both have gone through our high-performing leaders process and implemented our approach in their leadership. Instead of complicated, you'll find a simple, scalable, visual, and repeatable process for developing people and growing a team.

Our approach is easy to put in place. It doesn't require a considerable investment of time. It is sustainable over time and helps people grow and put into action what they are learning.

I could go on and on with other common mistakes I have made and those I have seen many other leaders and teams make. These mistakes cost millions of dollars. They cost leaders their sanity too. These are mistakes that keep leaders from growing, having a life, and a more significant impact on the world. For the sake of time, our relationship, and your sanity, I won't list them all. I will hit a few more common mistakes in a quick summary.

**Mistake 5: Complicated, top-down, strategic plans that are complicated.**

See what I did there? Okay, I'm all for an excellent strategic plan for a team. We create and implement strategic plans with teams of all sizes. But most strategic plans are very heavy on theory and very low on application. We've found only about 15% of people on a team typically buy-in to most strategic plans (a few executives or owners).

This top-down approach is exclusive, not inclusive. It leaves the remaining 85% of your team in the dark (everyone else). Leaving out 85% of people is not a good way to build a diverse, inclusive, and high-performing team.

Our process for developing people is very strategic, but it is also inclusive, eventually involving everyone on a team. It provides accessible, value-add leadership tools that every person on your team can instantly apply. The process works for entrepreneurs with small teams and for executives, middle managers, or front-line leaders.

Whether you have a team of five, 500, or 5,000, our visual and simple leadership tools will raise your team's entire culture over time. They will help everyone grow and help your team be more self-aware. When people are more self-aware, they will lead better, perform better, sell better and be better!

Our simple approach helps everyone on the team to bring their best every day at work. It also allows people to be healthier and happier moms, dads, friends, spouses, partners, and neighbors. Win.

*Healthier and happier people lead to a more productive work environment. Win. Win.*

**Mistake 6: Not data-driven.**

Imagine if you thought you had an infection in your arm. Now imagine I was your doctor. Imagine I walked in, looked at your arm, and immediately took out a saw and tried to start cutting off your arm. All without taking any tests, x-rays or anything. I had a Freddie Krueger flashback writing that sentence (80's horror movie reference). That approach would be insane for a doctor, right? But that approach is precisely what most leaders do with their teams and people. I call it leadership malpractice.

Without any data or objective insight, leaders hire influencers, virtual speakers, or gurus. They'll go to work on problems that they think exist, all without any real data to confirm their theories. This is exactly like a doctor trying to operate on someone without taking any tests.

Please don't do this.

In the pages to follow, you will hear about quite a different approach we take. You'll see a simple, data-informed approach to developing teams. You'll discover a better system that provides simple, objective data for leaders, and a measurable return on investment.

**Mistake 7: Hiring expensive coaches/consultants (wasting time and money).**

This one crushes me. Leaders throw thousands of dollars at consultants who have some of the darkest souls I know. Let's be clear; I'm by all means no saint. But there are so many leaders out there throwing money at consultants or coaches with no plan, little experience, or any way to realize a return on investment.

How do I know? I meet these so-called consultants or speakers at conferences and companies around the country. I hear them brag about taking your money and then sleeping comfortably at night with little care for you or your team.

I'm not trying to throw shade here. Well, a little. There are many unqualified speakers, coaches, or consultants out there. Many will over promise and under deliver any actual results to you, your team, or your cause. Most don't have any follow-up process, visual tools, or game plan for ongoing development with you or your team.

Don't get me wrong; there are great coaches and consultants out there too. I have met many of them working and partnering with leaders like Jeremie Kubicek (co-founder & CEO of GiANT) and others. These are real-life leaders with real leadership experience and real character.

They have a genuine heart for raising up more leaders around the world. And they have the credibility and capacity to back it up too.

What you'll also hear in this book are stories based on real-life leaders with real-life issues. These leaders have received real-life help and action. They've experienced real-life transformation, growth, freedom and impact.

You'll also see these gifted leaders engaging with dozens of practical and proven leadership tools. These are proven tools used by companies like Google, Ford, Chick-fil-A, the United States Air Force and many others.

To help you remember what you are learning, there is a chapter summary at the end of each chapter, written from my perspective as the author.

To help you apply what you are learning, we've also created a Development Plan for this book. The link is at the end of this chapter. You will want to check it out at some point to help process what you are learning and take action in the areas you would like to grow.

In the Development Plan, there is one page for each chapter of the book for reflecting, taking notes, completing exercises, and answering specific questions. You can even use the resource as a discussion guide if you are going through this book with friends, family, or co-workers.

# Summary

**This book is for you if you:**

❑ Want to grow and scale your revenue, team, and organization.

❑ Want to be more intentional about your personal and professional growth.

❑ Are looking for more time and freedom for the people and things you love the most.

❑ Want to develop people and see them win in work and life.

❑ Desire more impact in the world using your unique gifts and resources to change people's lives.

**This book is also for you if you:**

❑ Want to grow the leaders on your team but don't have a plan.

❑ Want to attract, hire and retain the right talent on your team.

❑ Lack a clear process for onboarding and developing leaders on your team.

❑ Lack practical tools to help leaders on your team perform.

❑ Are experiencing drama, miscommunication, or gossip with teammates.

❑ Want to build unrecruitable teammates that never want to leave your team.

❑ Want to have an engaged workplace where people show up every day and bring their best.

❑ Need inspiration from other leaders of what it takes to grow and help others succeed.

**This book likely won't be for if you:**

- Aren't looking to grow in your life and leadership.
- Have it all figured out, and don't want to help others reach their potential in their life or work.
- Are looking for theories and philosophies and not practical tools and resources.
- Don't want to grow your team, your revenue, your margin, and your impact.

In the next chapter, I'll share my leadership journey and why I wake up every day wanting to inspire and equip leaders just like you. In the following chapters, you'll hear stories from two different leaders dealing with real issues (Note: the details, names, and stories are changed to be respectful). You'll also see the impact of practical tools and leadership resources used by thousands of other leaders just like you around the world.

My goal is for you to grow in your life and leadership as you hear the stories to follow. I hope you find the freedom and margin you desire for the things, passions, and people you care about the most. Most of all, I want to help you maximize your unique impact in the world. We only get one shot at life, and I want to help you make yours count!

Go to <u>taleof2leaders.com</u> for the Tale of Two Leaders Development Plan.

# CHAPTER 1. 12 YEARS OF RESEARCH ON LIFE & LEADERSHIP

*Purpose is the place where your deep gladness meets the world's needs.  - Frederick Buechner*

I was a pastor and leader at one of the largest churches in America, a church my family still loves deeply today. It is tough to say precisely what it was that pulled me away from working within the walls of the church. I didn't intend on walking the path of empowering and raising up leaders out in the business world.

But with an entrepreneurial background and our own real estate company, my heart and empathy for leaders in the business world continued to grow and grow. It wasn't one single moment that got my attention. It was a combination of moments and conversations that fueled a passion for serving leaders.

Eventually, I mustered up the courage to take action and pursue full-time what I've been doing professionally now for the last season of my life.

Looking back, as a pastor and leader of pastors, I remember seeing the depth of desolation on people's faces all the time. Why? I saw the most desperation when people lacked real purpose or meaning in their lives. Unfortunately, that lack of purpose wasn't the exception to the rule. As a general rule, I have found the following to be true.

*Most people lack a greater sense of purpose in their life. Most people think or feel something is missing.*

You may have felt this way before or know others who are missing a purpose or deeper meaning in their lives. I felt this way for years as an entrepreneur and business leader earlier in my life.

One of my favorite authors, Donald Miller, explains how our lives are stories. And the difference between a good story and a bad story is the strength of the narrative driving the story.

Have you ever found yourself watching a movie or reading a book, and it's simply not connecting with you? The lack of interest or connection is likely because that book or movie has what is called a narrative void.

*A narrative void happens when the audience doesn't know where the main character is going, what they believe in, or what they are fighting for.*

A narrative void is what you get when there's no real purpose driving the story, and as a result, there's no real reason to engage with the characters in that story. I mean, who really wants to hear a story with no direction or purpose?

But far too many people and organizations are going through their days without meaning. Too many people don't know where they're going, what they believe in, or what they're fighting for. They are living and leading in a narrative void.

Let me explain.

Most people spend about a third of their lives working.

*A third of your life is a long time to spend without any real sense of purpose or meaning.*

Your job is not only a main source of your purpose, but there is a more profound sense of purpose and joy added to your life when you have meaningful work.

*We all like to be a part of a bigger story, a larger narrative. It is part of what makes us human.*

**Benefits of Meaningful Work**

Enjoying our work reaps several positive benefits. It gives us a sense of pride and a sense of accomplishment. We receive compensation when we work. That compensation adds value to our lives, our families, and our future.

Being in a favorable position in our work gives us other benefits too. Through work, we can find a sense of community and a sense of passion. Healthy workplaces can also offer mentoring, training, and inspiration. These are all benefits that make people's lives better.

As the pastor of a large, growing church with locations around the country, I met with many people over the years, hearing their stories about life and work.

It was like a twelve-year research project on people and leaders.

Most people like to talk about themselves, so I spent quite

a bit of time asking people about their lives and work. I asked  about their passions and their families. I provided coaching, mentoring, counseling, and support for many, many people over the years.

Over time, I began to notice a big theme about people's work.

For the sake of clarity, there were two main groups:

1) Those **with** purpose and meaning in their work, and

2) Those **without** purpose and meaning.

**The first group had a sense of purpose and found joy in their lives through their work.** I would ask what they did for a living. This group would go into a passionate explanation of what they do and how it gave them joy and meaning. It was so inspiring to hear from so many unique and talented people. Then something began to grab my attention about their stories.

Many of these people would point to their leader or the founder of their company. Then they would explain why they loved their leader.

I witnessed their eyes light up, talking about where they worked and the people they worked with. They would be so excited to talk about their organization's mission or how they are growing in their role. This was one group, and let me be honest, it was a tiny group.

**Then there was another very distinct group of people, those that did not have meaningful work in their lives.** I would ask the same questions, "What do you do for a living?"

But these individuals described their situation in a very different way than the first group. Most of the time, their entire countenance was completely different.

Some would say, "Oh, let's not go there."

"I hate what I do," another would say.

Some even went as far as to say, "Let me tell you why my job is the worst job in the entire world." Insert sarcastic tone.

Others even said things like, "Let me tell you why my boss is a complete and total nut job."

Some explained their inability to find work, which had a negative impact on their lives and families.

My background before being a pastor was leading my own businesses for around ten years. I've always had a heart for business owners and leaders. So when I was a pastor, I invited many people into conversations, asking them to meet at my office, their office, or to grab a coffee.

They would describe a difficult situation in their job or their lack of a good job. This group would talk about a leader or boss that they hated or a desperate situation that they were stuck in at work. This bothered me every time I had a conversation like this, which was often.

Many would go on and on about their long hours and their lack of passion. They would highlight the drama in their workplace, the toxic culture, or crazy teammates.

Some pointed out the amount of time they were spending away from their kids or their family. Single parents struggled to succeed in the workplace and lead their families.

Young people and married couples were desperately trying to balance their life and work with limited success.

*I spoke to so many people without meaning, hope, or anything positive to say about their life and work.*

Why was this the norm in the world?

I counseled a countless number of couples dealing with serious issues in their marriage or with kids. Most were good people inside, too. From a lack of hope to depression to anxiety or sickness, I began to link several of these issues back to the same source.

Most issues in people's lives seem to be connected in some way around their work, lack of work or stress from work.

I counseled kids whose parents hated their jobs. I lost count of the young kids and teenagers I met with over the years. Many had moms or dads that were absent in their lives due to work they felt stuck in or hated.

I counseled children dealing with addiction, drugs, alcohol, porn, cutting, bullying, abuse, or neglect. It may sound dramatic, but these are real issues I saw daily. I'm not naive enough to think there weren't other contributing factors at play. Still, one thing became clear.

*I could tie a lot of these negative issues back to a lack of meaningful work in our world.*

I would stay up late at night thinking about it. My heart hurt for these families and individuals. The emotion I felt for these beautiful people grew more and more intense. My mind would toss and turn, trying to figure out why this was such an issue.

> *Why was it so difficult for people to have*
> *meaningful work and a sense of purpose*
> *or even work they enjoyed?*

What could be behind this issue? Why was it such a problem? Why was the group that loved their work, their leaders, jobs, teams, and co-workers such a tiny group? Why was the group that hated their work, their leader, or their job so large?

**Experiencing & Developing Healthy Teams**

Almost every single weekend, pastors and leaders from around the world would come tour Life.Church locations. They wanted to learn about growth, organizational culture, innovation, leadership, stewardship, and teamwork. At the time, I was the pastor and leader at the Edmond, Oklahoma location. This location is where one of my long-time mentors, Craig Groeschel, now speaks and pastors weekly.

Today's Life.Church was a very different Life.Church than the one I went to work for back in 2007. What was then a small church with a few locations and employees had now grown to have a massive global impact. At the time of this writing, Life.Church is meeting in thirty-six locations in eleven states, with over a hundred thousand people attending in some way. There are hundreds of partnerships with nonprofits around the world, and the YouVersion Bible app has almost 500 million users.

In 2020 and 2021, Life.Church earned the number one place to work in small to midsize companies in the U.S by Glassdoor, which is quite an honor for a team of over 650 employees. Life.Church was recently named a Gallup Exception Workplace, given only to organizations meeting very high standards of excellence. I am grateful to have played a small part in the Life.Church story over the years.

It wasn't all easy seeing this organization and its leaders grow. I watched through the growing pains and the hard years. I learned from outstanding leaders like Craig, Bobby Greunewald, Jerry Hurley, Sam Roberts, and many others. Some of the best business minds in the world mentored me and taught me leadership.

I spent quite a bit of time coaching church leaders, non-profit leaders, and business leaders worldwide. I even had the opportunity to join the Central Leadership team and help drive this workplace culture at the many locations around the United States.

It was a dream job for sure. My eventual role on the Central team was to empower and mentor pastors, train leaders on team culture, and to reinforce the organization's values at the thirty-plus locations. I was also tasked with helping leaders to grow revenue and generosity, model financial stewardship, and help increase financial margin at physical locations.

I was still having a large number of coaching conversations with business leaders outside the Life.Church team. I loved these conversations, and my passion for helping leaders and their teams continued to get bigger and bigger.

We were hosting events for business leaders, and I wanted to figure out how to get leaders together to invest in one another. I wasn't just talking with employees, the first group mentioned previously. I was talking with the leaders of most of these organizations, the actual leaders most of these people were talking about.

Some leaders ran tech companies. Others owned law firms or manufacturing companies. Some were leaders in government and military branches.

I spent time in coffee shops, restaurants, businesses, factories, or video calls talking to or coaching these leaders.

At the time, I was their pastor. Somehow, the conversation always seemed to drift towards coaching them in their leadership or their work.

These men and women were just like you. They were dealing with leadership challenges, all kinds of drama, constraints, and cultural problems. You name it; they were dealing with it.

These were big-time influencers in our country! Through these conversations, a similar theme emerged as these leaders described their experiences. Again, there were two different and distinct groups.

The first group consisted of **healthy leaders with a deep sense of purpose.** This group of leaders seemed very focused, passionate, and engaged. Whether they were an entrepreneur, an executive of a larger organization, or a middle management leader, you could tell one thing: They loved what they did for a living.

You could tell these leaders were passionate, engaged, and called to their work. They had a sense of purpose and impact. Some of these leaders were giving back to the world in significant and measurable ways.

Like the workplace group that loved their job, this group

of leaders was a tiny minority. And like a giant sponge, I asked these leaders a million questions. Curiosity drove me, and I learned a lifetime of wisdom in exchange.

I wanted to learn and to help. Most of these leaders wanted to learn and receive help too. I was mentoring many of them in their personal lives. In a sense, they were mentoring me in their business skills.

Then there was the second group that consisted of **unhealthy leaders without a sense of purpose or impact.** This group was much larger than the prior. Most leaders from this group were stressed, burned out, and generally unhealthy in their leadership and teams. Many struggled to grow or scale their business.

Their personal lives or health were in shambles due to many years of neglect. The result was their influence and impact being so much less than it could have been.

*Many of these leaders were dealing with what they described as toxic workplace cultures.*

They had employees that didn't care and who wouldn't do more than the bare minimum. I heard stories of firings, turnovers, and team drama. Stories of miscommunication, missed goals, broken relationships, family drama, and financial hardships. No wonder they were so exhausted.

I spent hours and years praying for, coaching, and listening to their stories. I walked the halls of their companies and sat in rooms with their leaders. Some of these individuals could be great leaders, but they just didn't have the leadership experience, insight, or tools to succeed.

Many were technical leaders, doctors, lawyers, accountants, or contractors. Their technical skills as a doctor, an engineer, or a producer in their trade often did not translate into the soft skills of leading people. Most did not know how to build a diverse team, create a healthy workplace culture, or empower other leaders. Many did not know the skill of attracting or retaining the right talent. These were all skills essential to scaling their revenue, organization and impact.

At one point, these leaders loved their trade, but now they had to do their job AND lead people, which are two very different skills.

These were all things that seemed very natural to me because of my role and experience leading at Life.Church and as an entrepreneur and business owner.

Through the years, I continued to ask bigger questions.

> *Where are all the great leaders who could*
> *bring needed change to our society?*

Where were all the people who could lead through difficult, divisive, and challenging economic and cultural issues? Why are there so few competent, healthy, mature, and disciplined leaders? And why are there so many burned-out, unhealthy, broken, tired, overworked, and overstressed leaders?

I had met a tiny group of people who seemed to love their work, their leaders. Why was this group so small in number? There were so many others on the other side of the spectrum.

There were so many leaders without hope, without meaning, and without work they enjoyed. Why were these leaders the norm, not the exception?

*Why was there a shortage of leaders in the world?*

Yet, there I was on a team with a great workplace culture recognized around the country. For over a decade, I learned what it takes to have a healthy leadership culture and high-performing, yet dispersed teams.

I loved what I did so much and I loved my co-workers. But this burden and these questions continued to haunt me. The passion for answering these questions began to consume my thoughts. I felt an increasing sense of responsibility to steward my leadership and life experience outside the walls of the church.

One day, I was at a leadership event with most of Life. Church's top leaders. One of my fellow leaders approached me and asked if something was bothering me. Charlie was a great friend that knew me well. He could tell I had an internal battle going on in my heart and soul. Good friends can tell those things. In front of the team that day, some of my closest friends and mentors, I broke down in tears.

I opened my mouth and somehow words started to form. I just didn't know what those words would be. In some form of rambling, I mustered what was on my heart.

"I'm not sure what I am supposed to be doing," I said, "But it is time for me to head out into the marketplace again and go reach leaders with 100% of my energy and efforts. I have this thing burning inside of me to raise up more leaders in the world. It is time to do something about it."

Everyone was supportive. It happened fast. Did I just resign from my dream job?

## My Jerry McGuire Moment

Have you seen the film Jerry McGuire? There is a moment where Jerry McGuire (played by Tom Cruise) writes a manifesto on marketing. He emails it to the entire company. Then he stands up to leave his office for good with nothing but a goldfish in his hand. Everyone is staring at him, wondering if Jerry McGuire completely lost his mind.

Then he leaves the safety of a long-standing job. He ventures out into the unknown to follow a passion that was deep within his heart.

My moment was like that.

Except I wanted to pursue this calling: to help leaders like you grow and scale your revenue and teams. To help you reach your potential. To help solve this issue of the leadership crisis in our world. I'm called to help more people love their work and help influential leaders help people love their work.

I wanted to see more people like you impact the world, using whatever platform you have and making your unique mark.

I was so tired of seeing families and individuals hurt. I was sick of seeing so many people work their life away and lose their families and close relationships. It was time to help these world-changers realize their full potential.

To live it out in their workplace. I wanted to help these

leaders make a positive impact in the world. To grow their businesses, churches, and companies, and not lose their soul or families in the process.

So with the support of the Life.Church team, my friends and family, and others, I grabbed my goldfish and headed out.

# Summary

**In your work, which of the two groups do you relate to the most?** Are you working on a team that helps you find a deep sense of meaning and joy in your work? If so, great! In the coming chapters, I want to help you find even more meaning in your work.

**Or did you relate most to the other group, lacking a real sense of joy or purpose in your work?** Perhaps you aren't in a place that you love and, as a result, you may think you are missing out in life. If so, I know how you feel! Please keep reading or listening. I hope the stories that follow will bring a deep sense of hope and vision for you in your life and work.

**If you lead people, a team, or an entire organization, which of the two types of leaders do you relate to the most?** Perhaps you relate most to the group that showed focus, purpose, and joy as they influenced others' lives? If so, great! The stories and resources to follow will help you take your leadership to the next level.

**Or did you connect most with the group of unhealthy leaders?** Are you running on fumes, stressed beyond belief, or struggling to find both impact and joy in your life and leadership? If so, I don't think it is an accident to read or listen to this book. You will identify with the leaders in this story, in both their personal and professional struggles.

**I used to think the only way to learn as a leader is to make big mistakes.** I have made plenty and could likely write another book on the topic. Failure is a crucial ingredient to success. But you can avoid making big mistakes by learning from others. You can also avoid going down the wrong paths, by clarifying where you are in your leadership and where you are going.

**Use the Development Plan at the link below** to process what you are learning and get crystal clear on what you want the most right now in your life and work. You can also use the Development Plan as a discussion guide if you are going through this resource with friends, family or co-workers.

**In the next two chapters, you'll hear stories from two leaders: Ben and Hannah.** As mentioned, Ben and Hannah's characters are based on real-life leaders like you, clients we have worked with over the last several years. We've changed many details and stories to be respectful to our clients, but see if you can see your story in theirs. You'll also meet Jack, a helpful guide to lead them along the way. It may be obvious, but Jack is a fictional character representing my narrative voice in the story as the author.

**The next chapter is about a leader named Ben.** Ben owns and runs a growing technology company he launched in his twenties. What started as a small operation has grown into a massive movement stretching across the United States. He has been married for sixteen years and has a twelve-year-old boy and a ten-year-old daughter.

Go to taleof2leaders.com for the *Tale of Two Leaders* Development Plan.

# CHAPTER 2: I JUST WANT MY HUSBAND BACK

*Growth always begins with self-awareness.*

### Ben

Journal: A new day, another fight. It was usually about the same thing, again and again. I knew Claire was hurting. I could see it in her eyes. How could she not know that I was in pain too? I am doing everything I can to provide for her and our family, and it isn't easy! Does she think I really want to be working these long hours? I started this company from scratch. I can't just give up and abandon it now.

I'm in Kansas City this week for a job. Away from my family, again. I miss her. I miss my wife. I miss my kids. I miss the mountains. I'm thinking about the four of us sitting in a ski lodge by the fire, admiring nature, laughing at whoever fell the most on the slope that day. We haven't been on vacation in what feels like ages.

I am just too busy. My family deserves for me to be there, but my company needs me here this week. Nobody cares as much as I do. If I don't keep it up and running, who will?

I need help but haven't been able to find the right people. We live in the digital age, yet no one seems fit to help run a rapidly growing technology company. I am incredibly proud of what I've built, yet nobody else seems to be, including Claire. I know she just wants me home.

Sometimes I feel like an outsider when I am back there. They have all these inside jokes and memories that I don't even understand. I want to see my kids grow up; I want to make memories with them. I am too busy being a part of my employee's arguments and resolving my client's complaints. Change needs to happen, not just for the business's sake but also for my family. Just not quite sure how to change. I don't know what choice I have though.

I reached out to someone this week. I didn't know who else to talk to. I feel like I am done. My friend recommended I speak to a man named Jack Parsons. Jack helped him quite a bit in the past.

I was pretty skeptical at first, but I reached out and set up our first conversation.

I told him that I wasn't sure if I could do this anymore. I'm tired beyond exhaustion. I haven't seen my kids or wife in three weeks because I have been on the road putting out fires with my team and clients. When I am home, I'm not really mentally there at all.

Jack asked me what a win would look like to work together. Honestly, I wasn't sure at all. I had to do something different. I need more time with my family and less time in my business babysitting employees and putting out fires. What a bunch of babies I have!

He asked me a few questions. When we dug a bit deeper, I realized we needed a game plan to raise up other high-capacity leaders that can do what I do. Right now, I am a bottleneck. Everything runs through me. It is exhausting.

I know I need to hire more people, but it is tough to find good help these days. It seems like no one cares as much as I do or works as hard as I need them to.

To make it even more complicated, a lot of competitors are allowing their employees to work remotely when possible. This makes it tougher to compete and find the right tech talent.

I also want to continue to grow and hit 35 million in revenue this year, so we talked about our growth goals.

Jack asked if Claire would like to join in to provide perspective on one of our first calls. She helps with the business and seems to have good insight, so I agreed to ask her. The thing I was most nervous about? How honest she may actually be.

We showed up on a video call. I was out of town, so I was staring at my wife on a computer screen from the hotel, which was a bit awkward for sure. I guess it was better than not seeing her at all.

At least the continental breakfast that morning was terrible as usual.

Jack asked her, "If I was to work with your husband, Claire, what would a win look like in a year?"

She stared off into the distance. It was awkward.

Finally, she looked into the camera.

"I just want my husband back," she said.

We sat there in more silence. The silence seemed endless. I could see the pain and hurt in her eyes through the screen. I've known there is often a price tag for growth and business success. We were paying the price. I could see it in her heart and eyes.

It was painful, and did I mention awkward? But I knew I needed to hear it. When Claire spoke, she was usually right. I listened on. I would be working with Jack and his team. Still, I knew my wife needed to have ownership in the conversation, especially as a partner in our business. She was being honest, holding nothing back.

We came up with a few rough draft desired outcomes for the prospect of working together. Jack gave us a short exercise called The Wheel. It was designed to help leaders gauge how healthy they are in a few areas of their personal and professional lives.

Claire and I were to score ourselves in personal health, relationships, and a few other areas. Then when we get back together, we would compare results.

The Wheel showed areas of agreement (scores that are close by both parties). It also showed areas of potential growth (scores that are very different by each party).

Jack mentioned the tool was from an older man, a mentor of his. This older man invested in Jack's marriage when it was struggling years before. Part of me wondered if he would try to come in and present himself as another armchair expert. That wasn't the case. I thought it was good to hear his stories of struggle. As a company, our problems were something he had dealt with, and I was able to see a pathway of hope for Claire and me.

◆ ◆ ◆

I texted Claire this week and asked if she had a minute to talk on the phone. We talked through The Wheel Exercise together. She seemed cold and distant as usual. The conversation was a bit of an eye roll for me.

Why couldn't things be better? Why were things so different than they used to be when we first got married?

Below is The Wheel Exercise, along with my notes. Picture a wheel with five spokes. My scores:

**Spoke 1**. <u>Physical Health </u>- I would say I'm at a 5 out of 10 here. I'm tired all the time and not working out like I used to. I love being outside, and I don't get to do that as much as I used to.

**Spoke 2**. <u>Mental/Spiritual Health </u>- I would say a 4 here out of 10. I tend to get worn down quite a bit. I'm starting to forget things.

**Spoke 3**. <u>Relationships/Spouse </u>- Things are okay. 6 out of 10. Kids- 7 of 10. Not enough time, but I do get to spend some Sundays with them.

**Spoke 4**. <u>Work/Financial </u>- 8 of 10. I am somewhat successful. We cleared 25 million in revenue this year, which is not bad. A lot of stress comes with that due to all my work responsibilities.

**Spoke 5**. <u>Friends</u> - I'll say 1 out of 10. We are pretty isolated here.

This exercise sure didn't make me feel better about my

situation. I feel like I am failing in every aspect The Wheel asked me about, besides work. If this were an actual wheel, the wheel would certainly not be round. Several spokes were broken. I would be stuck in the mud, which is the way my life feels right now.

Claire scored our relationship at a 1 out of 10, and I was a 6. And she scored the relationship with my kids at 2 versus my 7. There were huge gaps between our scores and expectations in these two areas.

At least we are on the same page with the friends category. Both of us scored a 1 out of 10. She is alone. The only real "friends" in my life are at work, and most of them work for me.

A week or so passed, and Claire and I checked back in with Jack. When we talked, I was hopeful, but Claire seemed hesitant and withdrawn, which was normal. I mean, she had grown accustomed to me living and working like this for a long, long time. I didn't blame her for the attitude.

I expressed gratitude for her patience and willingness to meet up. We talked about The Wheel being off balance in several areas of our lives. I was spending all or most of my time and energy in the business, and my health and relationship spokes were very low. Claire shared her results too. We talked about the gaps between the scores and then came up with a few practical ways to improve the low scores.

I was starting to feel better about this exercise. It was quite liberating to quantify and put a number to how we were doing. This exercise took the pressure off of me and gave me a simple game plan for improvement.

And we could measure success along the way. Claire was still skeptical, but at least we had a plan.

A few weeks went by, and I met back up with Jack on another video call. He asked me a few questions. He asked me to imagine myself in the future, five years later. This activity was very uncomfortable for me, but I went along with it.

*"Just trust the process," he said.*

"Imagine that it is several years in the future. We've been able to work together for a while," Jack said. "Years have passed since that time, Ben. You have been able to do some of the things we discussed last week. Use your imagination. Close your eyes if you need to."

"Ben, describe for me what you are experiencing in that imagined future and what it is like. Be creative and see it. We are still on a video call, but pretend this call is five years in the future. We are reflecting back on today. Describe to me what you want to see in five years," he said.

I thought for a moment. Five years is a long way away. My phone kept buzzing in my pocket.

Slowly, I started to see pieces of it. I began to envision a future in a way I have never quite experienced, in my heart and mind. I started listing off the things we discussed the weeks before. I imagined what my life could be like in five years. He made me sort of "go there."

In my mind, I saw our kids as they were juniors and seniors in high school, about to graduate. I felt what it would be like to be close to them and close to Claire instead of so far away. I thought about being a part of their sports teams, their events, and me being around more during the week. I even imagined helping coach football or track.

It would be great to be a part of their lives. I thought about road trips together. I thought about knowing what is going on in their lives instead of getting updates from Claire every week.

I thought about what it would be like to feel close again to my wife, to feel respected, to go places together again like we did when we first got married, and not just traveling for work. I even thought about what it would be like to get an Icon Pass and ski one winter in Colorado or Montana with her. We've talked about the mountains for a long time, but we don't really go there any more. Life is just too busy.

*I imagined what it would be like to be in the best shape of my life, instead of tired, weak and stressed.*

I thought instead about being healthy and strong. I thought about Claire not being sick and anxious all the time. I thought of her not always having to be with the kids. All alone.

With work, I imagined what it would be like to have an actual leadership team and not flying solo, a team that I trusted to help me run my business. I dreamed about eventually being in more of an advisory role and less in the day-to-day operations. I thought about what it would be like to grow about twenty to thirty percent per year. I thought about possibly selling our brand someday and stepping back from the business or even starting a new one.

I called Claire that night as soon as I left our client's office. "You'll never believe the vision I had during my coaching session today," I said. I shared the vision with her over the phone.

She was very quiet as usual.

Eventually, I could hear soft tears on the other end of the line. I wondered if they were good tears or the other kind.

"I knew you had this in you, Ben. This is the vision I have always had for our marriage, our family, and our company. Your vision is why I married you. I know you can do this. I know we can move towards that vision. I believe it is possible, and I believe in you. Trust the process."

I hung up, and I went about my week. Soon, I started to have a fresher perspective on things.

I was on a job site with a government contractor in Texas. It was a massive contract for us. Our team was running tech projects across their entire base and throughout the U.S.

I felt overwhelmed as usual, but I had a new vision for my life and our company, one that seemed a bit more sustainable. It didn't revolve around me doing everything. I had a long way to go, but I felt like we were making slow progress. Trust the process. I guess that was my new motto.

The next week I jumped on my next call with Jack.

"Tell me about your vision, Ben," Jack said. "How has having a clearer vision for your life and business affected you this past week?"

I told him I had hope and that it helped. But I was a long way from making that new vision a reality. My phone never stopped ringing, and the emails kept pouring in. It seemed like everyone needed me to take care of everything every day.

"Okay, Ben, now you have clarified your ideal future, your vision for your family, and your business. Today we are going to identify what is keeping you from living it out. Sound good?" Jack asked.

"Game on," I said. I pictured the vision again in my mind. It was clearer than ever. I could see the kids in my arms as I was a part of their lives more than ever.

My phone was buzzing with calls while we met, so I silenced it.

Jack continued, "Thinking back to your vision, what are the false beliefs or negative thoughts that hold you back? What are the negative beliefs or lies that keep you from living out your vision?"

"What do you mean?" I said. That gave me time to think

for a minute.

"Well Ben, if you imagined your life in the future, what false beliefs did you have to work through and change to become the leader, husband, and father you saw in your future vision? What changes did you have to make to move towards that vision?" He asked.

I was silent for a moment. I knew what Jack meant, but I had never put words to it.

I silenced my phone again. It kept buzzing. It is always buzzing.

"It is all for them," I said.

"What is all for them?" Jack asked.

"The work, the hustle, the grind, the travel, the eighty-hour workweeks. I do it all for them. That is the lie I've been telling myself for the last twenty years."

*"I do it all for them," I said.*

"My dad was the same way. He 'did it all for us,' but as a result, I never really knew him that well."

I continued, "While I thought it was 'all for them,' it was really pulling me away from them. When I was home, I wasn't all there. When I was on the road, I wished I was home with them. I missed a lot of games and quite a few parties. I believed I was doing it for them, but my approach wasn't working. I need to make a change. So, in my vision, I made that change."

"What changes did you make? Looking back to when we started working together, what has helped you make that shift?" Jack asked.

We were imagining being five years into the future. We were pretending to go back to the present to describe what the significant changes were.

"I built a game plan." I said, "I had the support around me from other people."

*I went from being accidental in my leadership at work and home to being intentional.*

"I began to delegate more and trust my team," I said.

"Why was that so tough for you?" Jack asked. "When you said, 'I do it all for them,' did you notice the 'I'?"

"What do you mean?" I said.

"You said 'I do it all for them.' Ben, do you think you have to be the one that does it all?" Jack asked.

"Yes," I answered. "I've always been that way. Another belief that has held me back? No one cares as much as I do. No one has the level of detail and excellence that I have."

As we talked, Jack helped me to realize that the old approach wasn't working anymore. What got me to a certain point, those old beliefs, were now holding me back from growing. I needed to learn to let go. What got me "here" wouldn't get me "there." I wasn't letting go of control.

"Still looking back, what kept you from letting go of control?" He asked.

"I've controlled things for so long. It is what has led me to be successful. I guess I needed help learning to let go and have an open hand with my life and business. I needed help delegating, adding on other roles, and structuring the business model to run and grow without me. I just needed help changing," I admitted.

"Good. Let's make sure we are on the same page," Jack said. "The biggest shifts you made, looking back, were that you changed the story, the script in your head. Instead of 'I do it all for them,' you rewrote the script.

*To change the outcome of your story,*
*sometimes you have to rewrite the script.*

Jack continued, "You came up with a game plan for being intentional with your health and your family. In the same way you planned for your business, you made a plan to invest in yourself, your family, and your marriage. You learned to delegate to those on your team, to attract, hire and grow the right people. You learned to build a team and culture that could live past you, beyond you. Am I on track?" Jack asked.

"Yes, exactly," I said.

"And why weren't you able to do those things on your own? Why did you ask for help from me?" Jack asked.

"Well, it was pride, to be honest. I grew up to be more self-sufficient and not depend on others for anything. That is how we roll where I'm from," I confessed.

"I was afraid to ask for help, but I realized I wasn't going to be able to change on my own. I've been the same way, unhealthy, and pretty burned out for so long. I needed to change. I knew I needed something different. Claire needed something different. I'm a tech expert, but I have a lot to learn when it comes to leading people. I'm in over my head. I heard about what you do to help leaders and companies, so that is why I reached out," I said.

"Let me ask you this, Ben," Jack said. "Let's say it took two years to make those big changes. It required your time, energy, focus, and financial resources to hire me and my team and work together towards your long-term vision. Again, pretend you are there in the future, looking back on today. Was it worth it all?" he said.

"I would do it again a hundred times over," I said.

"Okay, I was making sure. What we do only works when people are 100% committed. It works when they are ready to make changes and ready to see their lives, families, and teams transformed. It is not a quick fix. It is a process. The process works, Ben."

"I can't do it all for you. I can only serve as your guide along the way. The process only works if you are ready to do the hard work and put in the effort. It sounds like your family is ready, and your team is ready. The big question is, are you ready to grow and trust the process?" He said.

"I am ready," I said.

"Okay, I'll get you a proposal next week," he said.

# Summary

**You can't give what you don't have.** Sounds simple, right? Here is what I mean. Before you are effective at leading others, you first have to learn to lead yourself toward health. Ben had to learn this lesson. You can't lead a group of other people on a journey that you are not willing to go on yourself. Are you ready to go on that leadership journey? The real journey begins with you.

**Growth always begins with self-awareness.** To get where you want to be tomorrow, you have to be honest with where you are today. Self-awareness is the key. We have to know what makes us tick and what it is like to be on the other side of ourselves. This is real self-awareness. We have to know ourselves to lead ourselves and others effectively.

**Intentional change doesn't come from accidental efforts.** Without a compelling vision and an effective strategy, you'll never get where you want to go. This vision and strategy are what Ben was missing in his life when he started on this journey. So let me ask you this question: Are you being intentional in your growth or accidental? Why or why not?

**Your personal life and your professional life are connected.** If you are struggling with one, it will impact the other. Pretending you don't bring your work home with you doesn't help anyone. Instead, it hurts your family or those close to you. Learning healthy rhythms with work will help you develop healthy relationships at home. Healthy rhythms at home will also set you up to win with work.

**Change is possible.** Often, we just need someone to believe in us and walk with us on the journey. And it can help to have tangible tools and exercises to help us ground ourselves in reality. We also need some sort of baseline to know where we are strong and where we need to grow.

**Are you looking to grow?** Check out the Development Plan at the link below. You'll score yourself as a leader and get clear on specific areas of growth. You also commit to a few action steps you can take today in your life and leadership. If you get stuck along the way, my contact info is at the back of this book.

**Looking ahead. In the chapter to follow, you'll meet Hannah.** I hope that you will connect with Hannah's story and learn from her experiences. Take note of where she is at the beginning of her journey. Check out the results of all her efforts towards the end of this book. I'm super proud of so many leaders like Hannah. I believe her story will inspire and challenge you wherever you are in your leadership journey.

Go to <u>taleof2leaders.com</u> for the *Tale of Two Leaders* Development Plan.

# CHAPTER 3: I'M JUST A _______ .

*If you have influence, you are a leader.*

## Hannah

Journal: I am so tired. Not sure why. Probably because I've been pushing and grinding every single day for the last fifteen years, going hard and trading my time for money with people I'm not even sure I like.

Our team keeps turning over people. We had to fire another new employee today for dropping the ball. Again. It makes for three people we have lost this month.

### Running on fumes and expressos

I (Hannah) feel empty, broken, and dark inside. Failure haunts me. Fear never stops chasing me. I'm so tired that I'm having trouble controlling my thoughts and mind. I've been drinking vodka a lot more too at night, which makes things even worse.

Honestly, my physiological state is out of whack. I am not sure how much more my body can take or handle. I'm pumping expressos and caffeine pills every morning just to get through the day.

The boys are not getting much time with their mom. They have a strong distaste for going to see their dad. He is such a complete idiot right now. It is like they are an inconvenience to him.

My body is not the only thing exhausted. My soul is tired too. I'm walking around so empty each day, struggling through each moment.

Help me, God. I don't know what to do. Help me find the peace that I am seeking. Help me to be still and present. Help me to see you and hear you. Why am I so tired and have so little energy? Why am I so drained and struggling so much? Why do things have to be so tough? Where are you?

Help me to know what direction to go, God. Help me to let go where I can and to hold tight to you. Help me to just breathe for a minute. Help me to inhale and exhale and breathe. My heart belongs to you. My soul belongs to you. My life belongs to you, God. But it is out of control.

I once loved the world I am in. I still love it, but I may need to walk away from that world for a while, maybe forever. It is overwhelming. So many people look to me, and I feel like a fraud all the time. Help me to know how to give everything to those who need me.

For now, I need to know what to do with the kids. Just make it work and go from there. To do list:

1. Rest up today. Try to go back to the gym.

2. Pick up the boys from their dad tonight. If he shows up.

3. Jump on a call with the NW region team to see what their deal is. Ugh.

4. Fire David for being such a pain for our clients and everyone else. Find another replacement for yet another role on yet another team.

5. Reschedule lunch with our managers, again.

6. Answer all the emails from sales and new employees.

7. Thinking about counseling or coaching or something. I can't keep doing this.

## Jack

Hannah was an operations manager at a regional construction supply company, a pretty powerful woman, living and working in what some would call a man's world. She was a super gifted and passionate leader. I (Jack) got to know her through a referral from another client. We talked casually a few times before.

Hannah sat at her desk with her head between her hands.

"Hey, I know it has been a very tough year for you. How are you and your boys doing? How are you adjusting to the new norm?" I asked.

"The divorce has been tough," Hannah said. "Our business is blowing up, but I feel like I am failing at every other area of my life. It is like what I am doing is empty and without purpose."

I heard this a lot from people during my time as a consultant and coach. It was the norm and not the exception. Most people I met lacked a sense of purpose and confidence.

"Can I ask you a question, Jack?" She went on, "How does it feel to be up on a stage or screen and speaking life to so many people in your work? How does it feel to have that much impact? It must feel pretty good."

She lifted her head and looked at me. She looked tired. I knew better than to say anything about it, but her eyes looked really tired. You can tell a lot about someone by looking in their eyes.

"I suppose so," I said. "It is pretty rewarding. I do get to see a lot of people's lives changed for the better."

"I wish I could feel that way about what I do," Hannah said.

I knew what was coming next, a line that I heard a thousand times over the years. This storyline broke my heart. I mean, I used to say it to myself over and over and over again when I was a younger leader in business, three short words kept so many from living out the calling on their lives.

Hannah spoke up again.

"I'm just a…"

She paused.

I waited.

I waited a bit more.

"I'm just a…manager at our business," she said through her hands. "That is it."

I have heard this so many times. The ending is similar, but the beginning of the statement is always the same.

People say some variation of: "I'm just…a manager. I'm just a middle manager. I'm just a CEO of a small company.

I'm just an executive. I'm just an operations manager. I'm just an administrator. I'm just a doctor. I'm just a pastor. I'm just a teacher. I'm just an entrepreneur."

"I'm just a...manager in a construction supply business," she said.

It seemed like most people thought the same about their lives.

"I'm just... no one. I'm just average. I'm just me," they would say.

I waited for a while for Hannah to say something else.

Eventually, she looked back up at me.

"Well, every day you wake up Jack, and you get to bring positive change in people's lives. You get to stand on a stage or show up on a screen and encourage and motivate people. You get to meet with and coach and inspire leaders on your team every day. You get to travel around and train and speak to teams. You get to help build workplace cultures and teams that people love."

"I'm just a partner and manager at a construction supply and management company. I literally sell concrete. The thing that mobsters tie bodies to so they will sink to the bottom of the ocean," she said.

My mind scanned for mobster movies to try and lighten the mood with a joke. Nothing seemed appropriate.

I asked her a handful of questions about her boys and her important role in their life. I asked about her company.

Hannah's organization sells materials to all kinds of different companies. They buy or lease parcels of land.

Then they bring materials in from around the country for construction firms and their projects.

Her once small construction supply company grew from 50 to 200 to 500 employees in a few years. They were experiencing major challenges because of the growth, too.

**New Perspectives on Influence**

Hannah was the operations manager of the entire organization. She was also a partner in the business. We did some quick math on how many people were impacted daily through her work. I wanted to challenge her to see her life, company, and influence from a new perspective. Here is a summary of what we came up with:

> Family members at an average of four people per employee (500 X 4): **2,000 people**
>
> Vendors and suppliers (500 X 4 family members): Another **2,000 people**
>
> Customers (1,000 X 4 family members): Another **4,000 people**
>
> Total people reached: **8,000 people**

"Wow. That is a lot of people! So, if I'm understanding," I said, "There are at least around 8,000 people your organization is regularly impacting."

Hannah began to sit up a bit more straight in her chair.

I continued, "Hannah, you are not only a conduit for construction materials and technology. There are thousands of people that look to your company daily for a source of income and jobs. These jobs give them a sense of purpose and belonging. They are now a part of something much bigger than themselves."

"Your company supplies materials to all your customers at an affordable price to run their business. You are also a conduit of business and life for all your suppliers and vendors. You add value to their lives, families, and communities. 8,000 people wake up every day and have a better life because of your business."

We added up the number of meals that her company was helping to provide for each family impacted.

8,000 people X 3 meals per day = **24,000 meals per day**

24,000 meals X 7 days per week = **120,000 meals per week**

120,000 meals X 52 weeks per year = **17.5 million meals**

Total meals per year: **17.5 million meals**

Then we estimated the approximate number of kids out of 8,000 people.

8,000 people represent about **4,000 kids.**

**4,000 kids are** getting three meals a day because their parents have work.

**4,000 kids** with a roof over their head and a safe home.

**4,000 kids** with a parent that has work and an income.

**4,000 kids** who have a chance to have a higher sense of value, responsibility, and self-worth. All because their parents have a good job.

**4,000 kids** whose parents are less likely to abuse them because they are less stressed about their income, and have a sense of meaning through their work.

I noticed Hannah's countenance begin to change a bit more.

"Wow, I guess that is a lot of kids, right?" She said.

"Yes! Let me ask you about your team. How many hours a week, on average, do you spend with your team?" I asked.

"Well, I usually work 70-80 hours a week, sometimes more," she replied. "I'm in meetings or calls most days with plant managers, suppliers, executives, and a few large clients."

*This woman was interacting with more people in a day than most would in a month.*

"What type of work do most of your clients do?" I asked.

Hannah shot back.

"It's just basic and boring construction: buildings, roads, highways, museums, schools, hospitals. You name a project in the area, and we likely supplied the materials for it or helped manage it. We also work through the Midwest, both large cities and small towns."

Her voice was slightly more enthusiastic.

"Okay, so let me get this straight. Your company has been a part of building a good part of this entire city and throughout the Midwest?" I said, "You have a direct influence of over 8,000 people that look to you, your leadership, and your organization. Your company doesn't just supply concrete and materials. Your company is also a source of belonging, hope, income, meaning, relationships, and service. And two boys at home are the most important of all 8,000 people. Let's not forget how big of an influence you have in their lives, too."

As I looked at her, the look on her face had changed entirely in the forty-five minutes we had talked. Her voice had grown from tired and cold to filled with a subtle sense of confidence. Instead of slumped in her chair and pouting, she was now sitting up, straight as an arrow. She looked much less sad, almost with hope in her eyes.

Hannah and I scheduled our next meeting.

My mind flashed to all the similar conversations I have had with people over the years. So many did not yet recognize their position of influence. I thought about the leaders who were struggling in their personal lives and leadership.

I realized that day none of those numbers or stats would ever be discussed at a typical strategy meeting. But those numbers matter because those numbers are people. And those people's lives are all better because of leaders like Hannah.

Like Hannah, thousands of men and women sadly thought the same limiting things about their lives: men and women out in the marketplace with more opportunities right in front of them than they could even begin to imagine. A world of purpose, meaning, and impact was just waiting to be discovered.

But instead of purpose and meaning and life, one prevailing belief dominated the airwaves.

"I'm just a ____."

I sat there in my office that day in a state of awe. I realized so many leaders in our country had this type of impact in the business world, government roles, education, non-profits, churches, and the marketplace.

Many of them had no idea of their importance as a leader in their employees' lives, families, or society. Many didn't realize this opportunity, and most were not stewarding their lives as well as they wanted.

*Many leaders want to have an impact and purpose in their work. Most just don't know where to start.*

I talked to way too many people every week that hated their jobs, despised their bosses, and had significant stress and anxiety about work. And as a result, they had all kinds of problems in their lives.

So many of these issues came from a lack of leadership in the workplace. I (Jack) felt grateful to play a small role in helping leaders like Hannah to get healthy as a leader, to grow their businesses and team and to discover and increase the impact they were having in the world.

# Summary

**You are never *just* anything.** Like Hannah, you don't just sell concrete, widgets, homes, accounting services, or surgeries. You are a change agent and a giver of hope. You are a conduit of life, meaning, and purpose for more people than you could ever imagine. You are so much more than you give yourself credit for. You are a light, a hope to the world. I hope you believe this truth today and don't ever forget it.

**Don't believe you are a leader? If you have influence, you are a leader.** If you have influence in your home, with friends or your team, you are a leader. And the person you have the most significant impact on every day? Yourself!

**The moment you say, "I'm just a ____," you are selling yourself short.** Please don't sell yourself short. As Jack mentioned, you are entirely underestimating your impact on the world. Ask yourself, who is right in front of you? Your closest friends and family. Your kids if you have them. Your team members at work. Your clients.

**Is it possible you are downplaying your potential impact on society?** Use the Development Plan at the link below to do the math. You'll take stock of all the people you interact with daily. Then, you'll write down specific ways you can intentionally grow in your influence. Whatever you do, please don't downplay the difference you can make in the world!

**Looking ahead: Next up, you'll hear again from Ben as he continues to grow.** I want to challenge you as you read or listen: Try to understand some of the issues he is dealing with. Do any of these issues sound familiar in your life, family or leadership? What about on your team? What can you learn from Ben and Hannah's situations and apply to your own life? I hope this book and the Development Plan are more than something you can engage with intellectually. Just like Ben and Hannah, I hope this is an experience you can go through.

**These are stories from people just like you.** They are dealing with the same types of issues you are experiencing. There is hope for you. You are only alone in your journey if you decide to be. I hope that you find encouragement for your situation and practical action steps you can take today.

Go to taleof2leaders.com for the *Tale of Two Leaders* Development Plan.

# CHAPTER 4: WHEN YOUR BABY GROWS UP

*We are all just prisoners here, of our own device. - The Eagles, Hotel California*

## Ben

Journal: It's been a few months since I started this new journey of intentional leadership. It hasn't been easy at all. Some days I feel like I am moving backward. Other days it seems as if I am taking a step or two forward. The personal conversations and exercises have been both uncomfortable and rewarding. I keep remembering these words: Trust the process.

### From Accidental to Intentional

I realized I've been reactive and accidental in leading myself and my family over the last decade. The cost is real. My marriage is hanging on by a thread. Some days, it is like I don't even know my kids. My business has struggled too. I'm at my wit's end leading so many people in a rapidly growing and ever-changing industry. I'm committed to the journey of transformation, though, and I am ready to change. I'm writing down the journey to track the growth. I'm also writing my story to inspire others to join me in the future.

## High-Performance Coaching Group for Leaders

This week I decided to jump into a coaching group for leaders with Jack. The group meets on a video call every two weeks and in person a few times a year. I was a bit skeptical at first. I generally don't love hanging out with other people I don't know, but this experience seems different and refreshing.

I am benefiting from Jack's perspective and leadership tools. I am engaging with leaders from various industries and roles. The group offers safe relationships and insight from outside my team. I can't be too transparent with those that work for me.

## Positive and Negative Tendencies

This week, we discussed leadership tendencies. These are our natural tendencies impacting our behaviors, actions, and our current reality. We all have positive tendencies that are hard-wired into us. Those positive tendencies lead to positive behaviors, actions, and realities.

We all have negative tendencies, too. Most of these are hard-wired into us from birth, from growing up, and from our adult work environments.

I realized this week our negative tendencies undermine our influence. Because of negative tendencies and actions, we lose credibility and influence with our families and our teams.

We learned a specific visual tool that helped us list our top two or three negative tendencies. Then we made connections on how these tendencies were limiting our influence.

◆ ◆ ◆

We discussed these negative tendencies on the call. It was eye-opening to hear people admit their negative tendencies and how their lives were negatively impacted.

To kick the call off, Jack went first. I thought this was helpful and opened the group up.

"Hey everyone, a great friend and mentor of mine has taught me many helpful things. One is to 'log' my negative tendencies like we are doing here. One of my tendencies is to say yes to too many things," Jack said. "A lot of people want my time, so instead of kindly declining or empowering one of our other coaches, I tend to say yes."

"The result is that I sometimes say 'yes' to good things, but I end up having to say 'no' to the best things: my health, my family, and my team. So as a result, sometimes I get worn down and don't put out my best content or work," he said.

I could see this issue resonated with a lot of the other leaders.

Jack kept sharing, "My friend also taught me the following truth, 'You can't give what you don't have.' But I was running on empty for a long time as a leader. Through self-awareness, I learned the following:

> *When we say 'no' to the good things,*
> *we have more time, margin, and energy*
> *to say 'yes' to the best things.*

"Okay, that is a tendency of mine. Now that you all know

I can tend to be a people pleaser, who else wants to share their tendencies? I would love to hear from the group," he said.

I could relate 100 percent to this one. I say "yes" to everyone, every time, all the time. I am worn out from trying to please everyone for the last two decades.

One leader, a hospital CEO, talked about a tendency to control things. He explained how he had a tough time trusting others. This negative tendency led to frustrated team members and a very slow pace in getting things done. I related to this as well.

Another leader, a very successful real estate broker, discussed a tendency to "over-sell" herself and her services. She was so busy talking in conversations with prospects, she had a tougher time slowing down and truly listening.

The broker identified the consequences of this tendency. She was experiencing a lack of connection with her team and with potential clients. She also came across too strong on social media, turning both friends and future business away.

I chimed in next.

"I can't believe the range of tendencies mentioned today," I said. "Sometimes it seems like I am all alone as a leader. Today, I realize I share a lot of the same tendencies as you all. One of my negative tendencies? I struggle to provide clear expectations to my team. I've been in this space for so long, and I often don't slow down enough to help empower others and set them up to win.

"I forget what it is like to be new in the role. I have sky-high expectations, but I don't share them. As a result, my team is often frustrated when they can't meet my high expectations.

"This year, I've lost two team members that I invested almost a year and around 200,000 dollars to develop. They text messaged me after their transition off of the team. Both of them pointed to the same problem: They were never clear on what the win should be. They felt like they could never win on my team, so eventually, they left to work for a competitor," I said.

I thought about a statistic I heard in our video this week. According to Gallup:

> *26% of employees receive effective ongoing feedback and communication.*

Only 26%? I wondered how many of our employees receive feedback and open communication. I hoped it would be higher than 26% of them, but I'm not sure it is.

"Any suggestions or thoughts for Ben or anyone else today? I would love to hear from some of the rest of the group," Jack asked.

"I have the same problem, Ben," another leader said. "I'm busy, and I don't take time to share specific expectations with our team."

"We have hired so many people in the last year, but we haven't had the time to go back and write down or review clear expectations. Most people don't even have a written job description or a clear win in mind," they said.

I thought of another stat from the video of the week:

*Only 21% of employees have performance metrics they are being held accountable for.*

Only one in five has accountability. Only one in five has a clear target to reach!

The group coached one another for a bit, and Jack chimed in at the end on a few points. We all walked away with a few action steps for the week.

◆ ◆ ◆

**Finding Your Tribe**

I was warming up to this tribe of leaders that came together to get support and perspective. It was fascinating to see leaders from different industries, time zones, and cultures. Each leader had their unique challenges, but many discovered that they weren't alone in their issues.

Over the following weeks, we shared practical, visual tools, adding immediate value to our lives and leadership. Because the leadership tools were simple and practical, we could take them back to our teams and immediately discuss and share them.

So we received benefits and accountability. Then, all those around us received the benefits and tools from the group, too.

Over the next year, I would jump on this short call every few weeks. The group would show up, bring their challenges and receive solutions. We all received coaching from Jack, his team, and other industry leaders.

This tribe of leaders had perspectives that I didn't have. These gifted leaders had real practical experience in law, accounting, arts, tech, real estate, and more. The people in this group were hand-picked to ensure they would be a good fit and add value to the group.

> *They were all wanting to grow as leaders of people, not just experts in their trade.*

There was so much combined experience in one place. I was able to show up and soak up that experience for an hour or so.

In addition to the group calls, I added in one on one coaching with Jack. The coaching was insightful and challenging in all the right ways.

Having accountability from an outside perspective increased my performance in many ways.

Some weeks, I didn't want the challenge, but I knew it was what I needed to get me out of my comfort zone and into a new level of influence.

I jumped back on our 1/1 call.

"You are like a personal pastor and business performance coach all in one, Jack," I said.

"Hey, that is the benefit of going through the process," he said. "But don't make it awkward."

We both sat there and laughed for a moment.

"Seriously, you are the one doing the work," Jack said. "I'm just showing you a pathway and tools to grow. This process wouldn't work if you weren't committed."

**The School of Self-Awareness**

"Ben, how are you doing on the tendencies you mentioned recently?" He asked. "Give me your top two negative tendencies and what you have done over the last two weeks to grow through each tendency."

He pointed to a visual self-awareness tool that showed the tendencies on a chart. Jack shared the following idea from a mentor of his:

> *We never truly graduate from the*
> *school of self-awareness.*

It is a continual process. This leadership tool we went through shows how your tendencies lead to patterns, which lead to actions. Those actions lead to consequences, and those consequences shape your reality. It is a continual process. We never really arrive. We never truly graduate from the school of self-awareness.

"Well, as I mentioned on the call last week," I said, "One of my top tendencies on my team is to under-communicate. I have high expectations and give high challenges to my team. But I give them a low amount of support or communication. They often have to figure things out on their own. I go from having high hopes to being quickly frustrated with them, never really guiding them to success along the way. I wish they could figure things out and didn't need so much hand-holding."

"Good, let's come back to that one. What is the other negative tendency you identified?" He asked me.

"Well, the other obvious one is that I work way too much. I'm a workaholic, Jack. I always have been. My dad was, his dad was, and so on. That is the way we roll.

"I remember when I was young, my dad would come home from road trips and light me up when I had a bad report card. Then he would just leave for days on end, like a giant bird that swoops, poops on you and then just flies away. He was always working. Always swooping and pooping too.

"I'm the same way. I don't know how to shut things down. Working from home occasionally makes it even tougher. You heard my wife say it. She just wants her husband back," I said.

I went back to one of our initial conversations.

"No one can do it quite as well as I can," I admitted. "Those are the lies I have believed for so long."

**Counting the Cost**

"As a motivation for you, how are those tendencies working out?" Jack asked in a direct sort of way. "Ben, do you see a connection between these two issues?"

"For sure," I said. "Because I don't let go of things and give them to my team, I'm in my head a lot. Being stuck in my head means I don't communicate with others as well as I should. So I have to answer more questions and in the end, work longer hours."

"I under-communicate on the front end, so we have to

over-communicate and redo things after the fact. More phone calls, texts, and emails, more time away on-site with clients or on calls. More time away from what I love. The team gets frustrated. Claire gets frustrated. Everyone is frustrated."

"Okay, let's talk about the first tendency," Jack continued, "the one to under-communicate and under-support your team. Can you elaborate on how that negative tendency impacts your team?"

"Well, as I mentioned, we lost at least 200,000 dollars on two team members that recently transitioned off the team. This number doesn't include the deals they took with them, which were likely another 500,000 dollars or more. These talented leaders had big potential, but they went to work for a competitor. I was so pissed," I said.

I thought about one of our previous meetings earlier in the week and a statistic Jack told us.

"Your stat of the week said this:

*Only 30% of employees believe they are given opportunities to learn and grow.*

"Looking back, I know we had high-capacity leaders that never have a chance to grow under my leadership. My tendency to under-communicate and under-support people pushed them away. One of them point-blank told me that in his text. Another employee we lost recently won a contract as our competitor. That one deal would have given us about a six million dollar tech contract."

*Our lack of leadership has cost us several million dollars of profit this year alone.*

"That makes sense," Jack said. "A lot of leaders we work with are only motivated if there is a high financial or personal cost. That motivation doesn't mean they are a bad person. It means there are only so many things that you can give your attention to as a leader."

"When the impact hits the seven-digit mark, most leaders can no longer ignore the problem. So I will help them see the million-dollar elephant in the room. It sounds like you have plenty of motivation now, so I won't rub salt in your wound," he said.

I thought back to all the other times this had happened and the millions we likely lost in a decade. There were likely several million dollars in lost people, time, resources, efficiency, and deals. I thought about all the time away from my family too, time I will never get back again. I can't even put a price on that.

"Okay, what about the leaders that are still with you?" Jack asked. "How does your negative tendency to undercommunicate impact them and their work?"

"Jack, we waste a ton of time and miss out on future deals. We don't have any real process or structure for communicating, so our conversations are all over the map. We are texting and emailing each other at all hours too. Especially on nights and weekends," I said.

"So this issue is negatively impacting your life, business, and your performance. It is also pulling your employees away from time with their friends and families on nights and weekends. The motivation sounds like it is growing. I know this is not something you planned. How much time do you spend outside of normal work hours emailing, texting, or working?" Jack asked.

"20 to 30 hours a week. At least. Sometimes less, sometimes more," I said. I wasn't proud of admitting this.

Jack kept persisting. "To clarify, why do you think your team is spending so much time communicating? What action could you take to avoid this big waste of time and energy?"

"I could cut out 80% of miscommunication if I would deal with the issue, slow down and explain expectations on the front end," I said.

"Yeah, but do you have time to do that, Ben?" He was trying to be as honest and realistic as he could with me.

"I don't think it takes a lot more time," I said. "It takes being more intentional with the time we have together. We have to learn to make the most of our time and be proactive, not reactive."

## Progress and Takeaways

"Let's make sure to get you a win for the call today. What are your takeaways so far?" Jack asked.

"Well, to be honest, Jack, I am working my life away, losing my marriage and trying to maintain control."

I sat there for a moment, thinking about what was coming out of my mouth.

"I am not investing in my team. We don't have a system for clear communication, leading to frustration and chaos. I am losing millions of dollars as a result. Also, I am negatively impacting the lives and families of my team. Instead of positively impacting lives in the process, I'm likely wrecking people's lives," I said.

I sat there in silence. This was a sobering reality.

"Another mentor of mine once told me this truth. You might want to write this one down." Jack said.

"He taught me the following:

> *You can have control, or you can have growth. You can't have both.*

"Think about that for a minute," Jack said.

He paused for effect.

"So which one are you going to choose, Ben? Are you going to choose control or growth? It is your life and your choice," he said.

"I want to choose growth."

Jack reminded me of The Wheel exercise I did with Claire to provide hard numbers and data. And we came up with a game plan to grow. He said we would be using a number of similar tools to score and track our team, to grow as a company, and perform at a higher level.

"Can I be honest with you, Ben?" Jack asked.

"Yes, go for it," I said.

"About your team, I hear you share a lot of assumptions," he said. "You think you are miscommunicating and under-supporting your team. You've lost team members and deals. Your life is slipping out of your perceived sense of control, which isn't real anyway. You have seen real deals and real people leave, but you need more than assumptions. You need data, like the data that The Wheel exercise showed you with Claire."

He continued, "I've been working directly with you. If we jump in and work on your team, we can assume we know the right areas to address. But without actual data, we don't know for sure the best place to start. Most of the time, I have found that executive leaders, like you, think they know where to start, but they don't. Why? Because you are biased. We all have biases, Ben."

"Most people won't tell you the real truth because they are afraid of your response as the leader. So most will pretend everything is fine, and they will deal with you and continue in frustration. And you miss valuable insight, feedback, and data from your team."

"Well, my team tells me when I am not supporting them," I said.

"Yes," Jack said, "but what about the rest of the organization? What about their teams? Is it possible that these communication issues extend outside of your top leaders?"

"Well, absolutely," I said.

Jack continued, "In my humble opinion, you need a reality check, a baseline. If you want me to work with your organization, we need real data to measure, track, and improve. I can tell you what doesn't work. Having me speak with your team one time will help, but it won't solve all your problems. And people say I am a pretty decent speaker too. More random, inconsistent training for your team? That likely won't work either. I'm not trying to be pessimistic, just honest.

"You need real data from your team to show you what is going well and what is not: real, honest feedback and data. Data needs a seat at your executive table. Do you have financial data and reports that show you how you are doing in your financials? Do you have numbers to show you where you are succeeding and where the trouble areas are?"

"Yes, for sure," I said. "Every month, we track those numbers and reports to see where we are doing well and where we need to improve."

"Great. You need data not only on your financials. You need data on your people and your teams. You are growing quickly and consistently adding team members. Your baby has grown up, Ben. The diapers just don't fit anymore. And diapers just aren't cute on twelve-year-olds. Your company is growing up. You must begin investing in your team's leadership and measuring the effectiveness of your efforts.

"You need data to show you where the baseline is: what is going well, and what isn't. That way, we can know where to start working. You think you have lost millions of dollars in team members, deals, and lost productivity. We will gather real data from your team and verify those assumptions. You'll know exactly what is going well and what isn't.

"Then we will give you a specific game plan to help you start working immediately on the areas that aren't going well. How would it make you feel to have a simple and scalable plan for developing your team? One based on hard data, keeping them engaged and helping them feel empowered?

"Jack, that would feel amazing, to be honest," I said.

"Great. Imagine your team enjoying their work more, gaining skills, and getting better in their leadership. Think about it. Do you want your team to feel so empowered they are virtually unrecruitable by competitors?"

"Does a one-legged duck swim in a circle?" I said. "Yes, let's do it."

"I promise you won't regret it. I will help you realize a measurable and tangible return on your investment. We will get started next week, and I'll talk to you then." Jack said.

We hung up the call, and I called Claire. She told me about the football games I missed this week. Missed a touchdown. I missed the parent-teacher conferences. And as usual, I missed all the other things too.

I hate that I wasn't there.

I had a major headache from the day.

But I had something better.

I had hope, anticipation, and finally a game plan.

# Summary

**Most people are accidental in their personal and professional leadership.** If you are reading or listening to this book, you aren't like most people! You may be like Ben though, accidental in your personal and professional leadership.

**Instead of accidental, the most effective leaders are intentional.** Starting today, how can you, like Ben, be more intentional as you lead yourself and others?

**We all have tendencies, most of which are subconscious.** Some tendencies are positive. Many are negative. In my experience coaching leaders like Ben, most leaders have no idea where their negative tendencies come from. And most don't know the negative consequences of those tendencies. What are your negative tendencies? Use the Development Plan at the link below to log your tendencies and discover how they are undermining your influence in life and work.

**It is difficult, if not impossible, to grow without self-awareness.** Without self-awareness, we have no idea what it is like to be on the other side of ourselves. What are you doing today to become more self-aware? It is time to find out what it is really like on the other side of yourself and your leadership.

**26% of employees receive ongoing feedback and communication.** As a result, most leaders are in the dark about where they need to focus and grow.

**21% of employees have performance metrics they are held accountable to.** The target shifts around like the weather, leaving people confused and unengaged.

**30% of employees believe they are being given opportunities to learn and grow.** This one kills me. This means on most teams, 70% or more of workers feel hopelessly trapped in their work, with few opportunities to learn, grow and develop. This is how Ben's team felt.

**Data needs a seat at your table.** Most traditional leadership and development efforts are not informed by data. Most efforts are informed by opinions and are subjective, complicated, and tough to measure. In the next chapter, you'll see how Hannah begins to use simple, objective data to inform her decisions. Regardless, if you are on a team of 5, 50, or 5,000, data needs a seat at your table.

Go to taleof2leaders.com for the *Tale of Two Leaders* Development Plan.

# CHAPTER 5: YOU HAVE A MILLION-DOLLAR PROBLEM

*Take ownership. Whatever it takes. No excuses, no explanations. - Tony Dungy*

### Hannah

Journal: I've been thinking a lot about my life and family. I'm struggling to survive right now, but I realize I have an opportunity in front of me, one I may not be fully embracing.

My boys look to me every day to be a source of life, truth, and love. Most days, I think I am failing. Honestly, I'm doing my best to just keep going.

I've thought a lot about the opportunity I have. I may have underplayed how vital my role is in the world. I do have so much influence, and I wonder if I am stewarding it that well. Lately, I don't think I am. I feel like I completely suck as a mom. If I am really honest, I don't think I was that great of a wife either.

At work, we are continually losing people in our company to our competitors. We have grown so quickly. I don't think I've been able to keep up with the growth.

I somehow need to step into my role as a mom and step up my game as a leader in our company. I'm not sure if I can do both well. How do people win at both? I'm not sure I can lead my boys through this tough season and have anything left over to lead so many on the team.

I can't stop thinking about the number of people that are under my influence. Since my conversation a few weeks back, I have thought differently about my role, our company, and the impact we can have in the world.

I reached back out to Jack this week. He owns a data-driven coaching and consulting organization, and speaks regularly with teams. And I knew he ran his own companies too. We have had a few helpful conversations in the past. I thought he might help me process thoughts from our last conversation.

## High-Performance Coaching

"I've thought a lot about what we talked about recently, Jack," I said over a video call.

"Awesome. I'm all ears. How can I help you?" Jack asked.

We caught up from our last conversation, and I updated him on the boys.

"Well," I said, "I've realized what a huge opportunity God has placed right in front of me. He has given me beautiful kids to lead and raise and a job I love with many people looking to me for leadership. I haven't stopped thinking about all the lives our company is reaching."

"I want to figure out a way to be more intentional and proactive as a leader. I tend to skirt problems and take shortcuts, like firing people or not dealing with issues. I thought I could talk through some of those issues with you," I said.

## Energy Vampires

Jack asked me about the top situations that were taking the most of my energy at work. I immediately thought of Sam. She is a total drama queen and is sucking up everyone's energy at work. Like an energy vampire, she sucks the life out of everyone.

"What?" I said. Jack was laughing. I wasn't sure why.

"I apologize, I just loved the energy vampire analogy," he said.

"Yeah, it is real life. Sam manages the sales team, many of which work remotely. All eighteen of our key sales staff avoid her weekly because of the drama she brings. A few even cited Sam as a primary reason for working remotely. I would have fired her by now, but she is the only one trained extensively on our current product line, which takes several years and professional trade certifications to really understand.

"Sam exaggerates everything. It can't just be a simple problem. Everything seems to be dramatic. She is so difficult. She is supposed to be supporting our sales team with data, customer needs, follow up and technology services.

"But dealing with her is a real whipping. Our sales team often avoids her or does the things she is supposed to be doing themselves. Sam ultimately slows them down, keeping them from focusing on their strengths. Our sales team should be 100% focused on selling our products and services to mid and large-sized construction companies, suppliers and municipal entities around the country. They aren't," I said.

"That sounds like a real issue," Jack said. "Let me make sure I am tracking with you. What I hear you say is on your front office and sales team, people are spending quite a bit of mental and physical energy avoiding this team member every day. Correct?"

"Boom. That's 100 percent accurate, sir," I said.

"And then on an ongoing basis," he continued, "Your sales team is not getting the support they need. They are not only spending time and energy avoiding this team member, but they are losing opportunities to serve their clients. As a result, you are missing out on deals, and your sales team is likely missing out on their goals."

"You nailed it," I said. "Also, I am spending a huge amount of time dealing with other issues like this and hearing the team's complaints. And I am making up for all the areas where Sam is dropping the ball. In reality, it is not just this one team member. There are a lot of other toxic issues on our team that people talk about regularly. Sam is just the first one that came to mind."

## Counting The Cost

Jack went on. "Let me ask another question, Hannah. Approximately how much of your mental and physical energy is going to this team member weekly and to issues caused by drama and miscommunication in general?" He asked. "Like what percentage out of a hundred?"

"About 30-40% of my time and energy go to dealing with

these issues and the drama, or following up with people on things I should not have to follow up on, or firing and having to refill positions," I answered. "It is embarrassing, I know."

"What about your team members?" He asked next. "What percentage of their time and energy is wasted avoiding Sam or complaining to you or one another about other co-workers?"

"I would guess at least 20-30% of their time," I said. "The team deals with Sam daily, so there is quite a bit of time that goes into the conversations. Again, there are others causing issues too. It is not just her."

Saying it out loud, I can't believe I have allowed issues like this to go on for so long.

## The Real Cost of Drama and Miscommunication

Jack responded, "I know your performance numbers and financial metrics motivate you, Hannah. Let's dig a little more and develop some ideas on how much these issues with your team cost you. Would seeing the financial impact provide you a bit of motivation on dealing with the issue?" He asked.

"Yes, definitely!" I said with some enthusiasm. "You know that is a big motivator for me."

"Let's start with Sam," he said. "What is her annual salary, including compensation and benefits?"

"90,000 dollars, if you add in benefits and health insurance."

"Okay, on a scale of zero to 100, what percentage of her job do you think she is actually accomplishing? I realize that is a pretty open-ended question," he said.

"I would say she is accomplishing less than 30% of her job," I said.

"Let's put a number on this," Jack said. "You are paying this employee around 90,000 dollars a year. She is accomplishing less than 30% of her job, which is a value of about 27,000 dollars."

"Yes, that sounds very fair," I replied.

"So you are losing at least 63,000 dollars per year on this one employee. This amount does not include the impact on you and the rest of the team. Would that be fair to say?" he asked.

"Yes, completely fair," I said, starting to feel even more embarrassed.

"Okay, let's talk about how this issue is impacting your personal sales productivity," Jack said next. "You mentioned you spend 30-40% of your time and energy dealing with drama and other issues."

"What is your personal sales productivity worth to this company per year? In front-facing client sales? In other words, what are you capable of producing in a year? I realize that is a very personal question, but again, this will help motivate you to want to make some changes," he said.

"Well, in front-facing client sales alone, I create just a bit. I produce between half a million and a million dollars in annual sales profit with a few key clients," I said.

"So this doesn't include the rest of your team, only your personal production, right?" He asked.

"Yes, depending on the year, that is what I can bring in," I said.

"Let's be conservative and go with the low end, 500,000 dollars. 500,000 dollars is what you are capable of producing on the low end. You spend 30-40% of your time and energy dealing with team drama, fire-fighting, and gossip.

"I realize this is a guesstimate and not exact numbers, but 30% of 500,000 dollars is 150,000 dollars. So the time you are spending putting out fires, listening to gossip and drama, or dealing with this employee is costing you at least 150,000 dollars. Is that a safe bet?" He asked.

"Yes. I would say easily 200,000 dollars because I know I can hit a million in annual sales profit, so 200,000 dollars would be very conservative. This amount doesn't even include the sales team I lead personally. This one team is bringing in between ten and twenty million in commissions per year. And they could be doing more if they had more support. We have other teams too," I mentioned.

"Makes sense," Jack said. "Now, let's add 200,000 dollars from your production to the 63,000 dollars she costs you on salary and benefits. This issue alone is costing at least 263,000 dollars per year or roughly a quarter of a million dollars.

We haven't even looked at the precious time the rest of your team spends dealing with this one team member. With eighteen team members alone on your main office team, I imagine these issues are costing you a lot of time and money."

Here were my notes from the rest of our conversation:

Sam's Salary and benefits: $90,000  X 30% (of her doing her job) = **$63,000 loss** in productivity

My Personal Production:  $500,000 / yr  X 30% (time dealing with drama, etc) = **$150,000 loss** of productivity (conservative estimate)

Team Salary: $2,000,000 / year X 30% (energy dealing with drama, conflict in general): **$600,000 loss** of productivity

Two team members lost to competitors: **$500,000 loss** in revenue

Total potential loss in productivity: **$1,000,000 plus loss** per year

**The Million Dollar Problem**

"Okay, Hannah, so we are clear that there is a huge problem on your team. In your mind, your problem starts with this individual but then extends out to the rest of the team. This issue has cost you at least a million dollars per year over the last few years.

*You have a million-dollar problem.*

"You realize this is a big issue on your team, and you have tried a few things to fix the issue, but it is still a significant problem. Let's talk about what you have tried to do to fix these issues on your own." Jack said.

I thought about it for a moment.

"Well, I've tried a lot of things," I told him. "We brought in a motivational speaker last year. He spoke on teamwork and the value of serving the team and clients. Everyone loved it, but after a few weeks, we didn't see any changes.

*People forget most speakers' content and go right back to their old habits at work.*

"I have talked to this employee and others: gossip and drama are problems on our team. I don't have the time and energy to follow through. I don't love conflict, to be honest, so it is easier to pretend it is not there and pray that it will go away. Sometimes, I let issues go for so long, I will eventually lose it and blow up on people." I said.

"Well, that sounds intense. So you have brought in speakers that weren't too great. They didn't provide any follow-up tools, visual resources, or anything digital to reinforce their topics. You've talked with team members about it, and had team conversations. Occasionally, you'll drop a virtual hand grenade on someone, blowing them up to prove a point. Anything else you have done?" He asked.

"Well, we used to have weekly team meetings together. We would listen to a podcast, or I would share a talk. I was spending way too much time coming up with talks or podcasts, so we got out of the habit. They were differ-ent every week, and we didn't gain any real traction over time. It was a bit of a popcorn approach," I said.

"Okay, that makes sense," Jack said. "So you have spent time, energy, and effort to try many things, and none of them have helped. You realize there's a huge financial cost. Your team morale is low. It has been worse in a partially remote work environment.

"The problem  is not just one team member, but you have more significant issues with other team members. These issues are costing you millions of dollars in lost productivity,  morale, and opportunity.

"As the leader, you are realizing this is your responsibility and problem to deal with. And you are wanting to now take ownership of the problems. Is that correct?"

"Blunt, but true," I said.

"You have tried for a long time to fix these issues on your own," he continued, "or with other speakers or consultants, but you haven't seen change or results. Again, the issues have cost you at least a million dollars a year or so."

"Again, true," I said.

"Additionally, you want to be a healthy leader not just for your team but for your boys at home. You contacted me because of our recent conversations and because your friend has spoken highly about our work. I'm 100% confident we can help you with the issues you mentioned," Jack said.

"What if I could show you a plan that resolves a lot of these problems over time and helps you grow your team too? It gets you your sanity back and helps you get healthy as a leader and have more margin for your family. And takes the pressure off of you as a leader to have to come up with a plan, giving you a proven process to grow your team, would that be helpful to you?"

"Helpful? It would be a miracle," I said.

"Great," Jack said. "We will give you a plan based on data, not assumptions, and scalable to your many locations. It's a proven process we've used with hundreds of other companies, not based on fluff or theory. Our process is measurable, meaning we measure your team's actual engagement and performance on the front end. Then we'll re-measure as we go to track actual progress. We'll focus on pain point areas and track real results with the team as well as financial impact."

"Yes, that would be extremely helpful, and I am willing and ready to do what it takes to grow our team," I said.

"Are you sure?" Jack asked. "Because what we do requires effort and commitment. You'll see an immediate impact when we start working together, but it takes at least 12 months to see big results. Most of our client work lasts at least 12-24 months. It is not complicated. It is simple. But it's not easy. We only have real success with committed leaders who want to see lasting change, not quick fixes. Our process only works when you want to invest in your team and care for people over the long haul."

"Yes, I'm ready. When can you send me a proposal and get started?" I said.

# Summary

**Regardless of your work or life, you, like Hannah and others, have an opportunity for influence.** How will you use that opportunity? How will you use your life for influence? I don't know about you, but I want to make the most of my life! I've been able to help leaders like Hannah and many others, and I want to help you do the same.

**Where attention flows, energy goes.** Like water, your energy as a leader flows to the lowest places on your team. Like Hannah, there are likely issues draining attention and life from your team. How is that working out for you? What is your plan to identify and help these leaders? Imagine having new energy to spend on other opportunities. What would that energy be worth to you?

**Look at yourself first.** Before pointing fingers, ask yourself, "What have I done or not done to set those on my team up for success? Have I been clear? Have I provided the right amount of support to help them win?" The best leaders take ownership of both struggles and wins. It is what leaders do. Own your mistakes. Start with yourself and go from there.

**As a leader, if you don't deal with the problem, you become the problem.** Ensure that you are doing all you can, and give all the right support. Provide clear expectations and resources to help others win. Decide to solve problems, not ignore them. If you are the leader, it is your job to deal with problems. It is what leaders do.

**Don't put off until tomorrow what you need to deal with today.** Decide today not to ignore the small issues. As you grow, the problems will only grow with you.

**According to our research, most teams function at 58% of their potential.** Why? Most people on a team feel undervalued or taken advantage of, or misunderstood. As a result, most team members don't bring their best in their work. At a 1,000,000 dollar payroll, this means most teams are getting around 580,000 dollars in value. This low engagement is a big problem as well as a poor return on investment.

**Google says, for every five teams in an organization, you have a million-dollar problem.** (Annual lost revenue = underperformance + turnover cost). How many teams are in your organization? Use the *Tale of Two Leaders* Development Plan to estimate what underperformance and low team engagement may be costing you. If you care about people and growing your revenue and team, the simple exercise on the Development Plan should give you plenty of motivation to grow.

**In the next chapter, you'll hear again from Hannah** and get a front-row seat to her growth and development. Watch as she identifies what is holding her back and see what steps she takes to get more of what she wants in her life and leadership.

Go to taleof2leaders.com for the *Tale of Two Leaders* Development Plan.

# CHAPTER 6: FINDING TRUE FREEDOM

*You can't give what you don't possess.*

## Hannah

I joined a coaching group for leaders this week. Part of our assignment was to write down my brief thoughts in a journal or on a laptop. I'm still tired, and journaling is a stretch to keep doing. But I know it is good for me. It is helpful to have a place to get thoughts out of my head.

◆ ◆ ◆

**High-Performing Coaching Group for Leaders**

On the video call this week, Jack asked the following question: "What are you trying to prove?"

This question hit me hard. Like right between the eyes. What am I trying to prove? What am I not trying to prove? That I can win as a single parent? That I can be a successful executive and run a fast-growing national company?

His question haunted me all week. Everything I did came from an effort to prove myself.

As a woman, I have dreamed my whole life of making

a difference in the world. I realized something on our coaching call last week.

I have been looking to others to find my real value. Instead of looking within, I'm seeking the approval of others by striving so hard to succeed.

Where does this come from, this relentless pursuit for more?

Every leader should ask this question:

*What are you trying to prove?*

What am I trying to prove? I flashed back to growing up.

I saw myself at eight years old as a young girl.

Things were tough at home. My mom was busy dealing with her own issues. She didn't notice me most of the time.

I felt invisible, like discarded laundry that no one wanted to deal with. A lot of times, I was alone, but I still had to figure things out in life.

One year, my mom gave me a red dress for my birthday. When I wore that dress in our dirt-filled backyard, I felt important. I felt like a million dollars. There was something about that red dress!

But most of the time, as a young woman, I did not feel valuable.

This was the way things were. You just didn't feel valued.

To be honest, I don't think I ever stopped striving to find this value and prove myself. I worked hard through college. I studied my way through engineering school. I jumped into materials and construction, an industry dominated by men.

I realized this week a humbling truth about myself:

*There is something dark behind
every text message I send.*

Behind every email that goes out, insecurity creeps in the background. Even when I speak at events or online, it continually whispers in my ear, telling me I don't have what it takes.

To this day, I'm still trying to prove my value and worth to the world.

Like that little eight-year-old girl in the red dress, I am still striving to be valuable. And noticed.

As a result, I over-correct through my work.

I'm still trying to show everyone what I bring to the table. This insecurity comes out each time. Every. Single. Interaction.

No wonder people seem so distant from me.

When I lead a meeting, I'm the technical expert. I always point to my technical knowledge of the materials and engineering world. This knowledge impacts my influence and has gotten me to where I am in my career.

But today feels different. I don't think that desire to prove myself is serving me well anymore. It seems like now it is holding me back instead.

I had my 1/1 call this week with Jack and shared what I

was learning about myself.

## Negative Tendencies & Negative Consequences

"I'm learning about a tendency to prove myself to the world and others through my performance. There are so many great things about my drive and work ethic. I guess I wouldn't be successful without that hustle and drive."

"But deep down, there is a relentless desire inside, constantly telling me I am not enough. I still find my value as a woman through two things: my work and others' approval. That need has never gone away," I said.

"How are those tendencies serving you today, Hannah? How is the tendency to prove yourself shaping your current reality?" He asked.

"Oh, there are major negative consequences," I said. "I know the tendency isn't serving me well. I'm coming to terms with each tendency and where they all come from. People see me as a bit of an elitist."

My heart was beating fast, and my eyes were welling up with tears.

Why was I feeling so emotional? I went on.

"No one can live up to the standard I have set in our company. Excellence is a good thing in our world, but I tend to take everything to the extreme," I said. "As a result, people keep me at arm's length, knowing they can never really live up to my high expectations. I've even asked a few people I trust over the last week to share their feedback with me about my leadership," I said.

"They hardly said a word."

"You are great," one leader said.

"Great? Great doesn't mean great. Great means you don't trust me at all. These three shallow words were the most they could muster?" I thought to myself.

My eyes started watering.

Then tears began to stream down my face.

"Great feedback," I thought. "So helpful. Insert sarcasm."

Jack sat there listening on the screen. I went on.

"My teammates have always seemed very distant. It seems like they don't feel as open as I would like for them to be about issues on their teams. They seem timid to share the truth, and I have to pull it out of them," I said.

I sighed and took a deep breath. You can do this.

**Saying you are good when you are far from good**

"Feel free to take a minute if you need to," he said.

"I'm good," I shot back.

That is what I say to people when I am not good. I lie and say I am good. Then I keep hurting.

I sat there thinking about how I want people to be open and honest, but I couldn't even be honest at this moment. What a hypocrite.

"When I dig a bit deeper and keep asking the tough questions, I realize that many people feel intimidated by me.

They rarely speak up on our team. I mean, the last one that was openly honest was fired the next week. I wonder if people feel like they can't be honest with me. We are a very fast-paced company and are expanding to states around the country. We are currently the top materials supplier in this part of the country. Soon, we'll be the number one supplier nationwide," I said.

"Okay. Can I ask you a pretty raw question?" Jack said.

"Yep, I am an open book," I said. As usual, I wasn't sure how open I really wanted to be. Or how honest.

"It sounds to me like that desire to find your value in your work or the opinions of others served you well for some time. You used this to drive you, and you have been incredibly successful. But you now realize that there is a dark side to that tendency to prove yourself. As a result, you've experienced quite a few negative consequences that are holding you back. They seem to be holding your team back too," he said.

"Hannah. Listen to me," he said.

Jack paused.

"Hey...you don't have to live like that anymore," he said.

**Finding True Freedom**

A few moments passed.

I was very still and quiet.

"Hannah, now you recognize the negative tendency, and

you can choose a different way. It is not who you are. It is a choice. You know that, right?" He asked.

I sat quietly. Then, I nodded.

I was so emotional, I could barely speak.

Jack continued, "You now know that you can find your value in who you are, not just in what you do. Out of the personal freedom and release of pressure to prove yourself, you will experience a new joy.

"When you find real freedom, you will experience a new sense of hope, a new sense of intimacy with your friends, your kids, and your co-workers. And as a bonus: a new love for life.

"Life is way more fun when you aren't walking around with a need to prove yourself every day. Are you ready to let that go of that pressure you are putting on yourself and start living a new kind of life, Hannah?" He asked.

I was emotional and felt pain in my heart. I was literally shaking. I felt like all the weight and pressure I have put on myself my entire life was pushing down on my shoulders. Like a thousand pounds of pressure, pushing down on me in that moment.

I opened my mouth, not sure what words would come out.

This was hard.

"Yes. I am so ready."

# Summary

**What got you to today likely won't get you to the next level.** Like Hannah, all of us have long-held beliefs and patterns of behavior. What may have served you to a certain point or helped you get to where you are in the past season won't necessarily help you or serve you well in future seasons. What you have done well in the past may actually be holding you back today.

**You can't give what you don't possess.** If you want to grow your business, a team of people, find more margin for what you love or have a more significant impact in the world, there is only one place to start: you. You can't give to others what you don't already have. If you want teammates that are growing, make sure you are growing in your life and leadership. Do you have a game plan for personal and professional growth? I hope so!

**Most people look outside of themselves to find their value.** In the end, looking "out there" will only leave you feeling more frustrated and empty, like Hannah. Finding value in performance and success is a relentless pursuit. This approach will only lead to short-term fulfillment. Instead of "out there," look "in here" and take steps to discover who you really are.

**Ask yourself the tough questions.** Use the Tale of Two Leaders Development Plan to discover the following:

- Negative beliefs and tendencies that may be holding you back.
- Opportunities for more energy, margin, and freedom.
- How negative tendencies are shaping your reality.
- Action steps for growth for you and your team.

**In the chapter to follow, we'll continue along with Hannah and Ben's story.** Note how they are becoming more self-aware and taking action steps to get more of what they want in their lives.

**Learn from Google and others.** In the following chapters, you'll also learn how companies like Google are using better data and insight to build high-performing people and teams in the 21st century. We'll share examples that you can apply to your own life and situation.

Go to taleof2leaders.com for the *Tale of Two Leaders* Development Plan.

# CHAPTER 7: DO YOU KNOW YOUR LEADERSHIP BASELINE?

*There is nothing to prove and nothing to protect.
I am who I am and it's enough. - Richard Rohr*

## Hannah

A few moments passed. I can't adequately put into words what happened next.

I can't explain it, but at that moment, I felt a calming sense of peace come over my mind and my body.

In my heart, I felt a release of pressure to prove myself. The weight I was feeling a few moments before was gone. The pain wasn't as intense.

Something was happening to me. I'm still not sure what.

There was something powerful about speaking those words and making a decision to let that part of my life go.

What I experienced next was an unexplainable peace.

"Hey, feel free to take a few minutes. I realize we are processing a lot here Hannah," Jack said.

"Yeah, can you give me a moment?" I asked.

I excused myself. Then I came back to my laptop.

"How are you doing?" Jack asked.

"Good, actually. Sorry. Just a lot of emotion bottled up there," I said.

I think I was even telling the truth this time.

"I am a vault," he said. "Don't worry. I've heard worse."

We both laughed. I took a deep breath.

I needed to hear that. I felt like such a basket case at that moment.

## Challenging Assumptions

We connected the following week. After catching up, Jack asked me a few questions about our team.

"Hannah, you've shared a lot of assumptions with me. Would it help for you to have specific feedback from your team to help you know if your assumptions are correct? We can give you black and white numbers to show you where your teams are doing well and where they are struggling."

"We can take the guesswork out of leadership development and help you know where to put energy, and not put energy, so you can focus on growing your company. Would this be helpful?" He asked.

"Yes, absolutely," I answered.

"Okay, we can take your team through a very simple ten-minute assessment. Our assessment measures five areas of team performance. Google determined these five specific areas contribute to their highest performing teams. They did a two-year study and spent millions of dollars, so you wouldn't have to."

He had my attention.

Jack continued, "Our assessment comes from this study and we've used it with hundreds of teams like yours. It will show you exactly where you are healthy and where you can grow as a team. It will also show you specific performance data listed out by your individual teams. We'll assess your team. Then we introduce specific tools and language to help your team grow in each area."

"We have a proven plan we've been tweaking for years. We'll start to work on the plan right after we take the assessment. Then we reassess every three to six months to measure progress. The improved scores will help to show you a tangible return on your investment."

If this could help me realize the type of leader my team thought I was, I was interested. If it helped us to grow and gave me time back, I was all for it.

**A Leadership Baseline**

"You have financials you review every month with your teams. Now you will have a way to measure the performance of your people and your leadership. It is simple and scalable at any of your many locations.

"Most importantly, it is practical. Before we assess the team, I will often lead the team through a short, virtual Leadership Bootcamp. We connect as a team and invest in your leaders to help them be more self-aware. Then I talk one on one with key leaders to give them practical insight on their leadership," he said.

"I will meet with key leaders because we are talking about real people here. Data is helpful, but I want to get a feel for how the team is doing and how we can really serve you and your team to help you hit your goals.

"Generally speaking, I'm a safe place for these leaders to talk with, and usually, people are sincere. Sometimes, it takes a bit of time for them to open up. After we do a team exercise together to increase communication and get your leaders a few quick wins, they'll be even more open to working together," he said. "You will have insightful data for your team too."

"Like a baseline?" I asked.

"Yes, this will give you a leadership baseline to measure reality. To celebrate and to improve," he said.

"Great," I said. "Let's do it!"

It's been a few days since I've talked to Jack. Today's assignment is to write down my tendencies. We all have both positive and negative tendencies.

*Our tendencies impact our actions, which in turn have both positive and negative consequences. Those consequences shape our reality.*

I've been writing down my positive and negative tendencies. One of my negative tendencies is that I overcompensate for not feeling valuable. I have a need to prove myself, so I overwork and overdo everything. I know this negatively impacts the team. People are exhausted.

One team member told me recently I was intimidating. He said working with me was like working with Michael Jordan, the NBA basketball legend, a.k.a. super intimidating. He said he felt like he could never live up to the standard that I have set for myself and the team. Ouch.

It is the same way with my boys at home too. I feel like I am so hard on them that they can never do it all right. I know this because they have told me.

Recently, I corrected the boys for correcting each other. Then, I realized they were simply doing what they see me doing, which is correct them all the time!

Through the team exercises, I realize the team doesn't trust one another as much as I thought. There is quite a bit of bickering and complaining, and you could feel the tension in our time together. That stuff drives me crazy.

Still, I am excited to have the support and a fresh perspective from outside of our team to walk us through this journey. I believe the following from my time as a leader:

*It is tough to read a label from inside the bottle.*

Sometimes it just helps to have an outside perspective.

This process is not easy, but I am starting to see the light at the end of the tunnel.

# Summary

**Google spent two years and millions of dollars** and found the following to be true: Teams with psychologically safe environments had team members that were less likely to leave. These teams valued diversity and were more successful too. A team that doesn't trust each other doesn't perform, which has substantial financial consequences. We've reshaped the five categories with different vocabulary. But if it is good enough for Google, it is good enough for us!

**Most teams have data to measure financial growth.** Few teams have data to measure people and performance growth. Unfortunately, leaders make massive decisions and spend millions on technology and assets without subjective data on their leadership and people.

**Leadership is such a buzzword in our culture** (so is the word "culture," by the way). Leadership is so subjective. There are a lot of opinions out there. Every leader I know, including myself, is biased in the way they view their own leadership. Leaders need objective data to help inform decisions.

**Most teams score low in communication and relationships.** As a result, leaders don't always hear the truth from those they lead. Many of us view ourselves way too generously. It is tough to see our blind spots and shortcomings as leaders. Having the right data helps us to make leadership less subjective and more objective. Black and white data informs us and helps us lead and develop our most important asset: our people.

**What you measure grows.** The older I get, the more I have found this to be true. Do you, like Hannah, want to develop your leadership and your people? Measuring your leadership and your team's growth is the best place to start. Everyone likes to have a target to hit. And not just numbers, or financials, but a tangible way to track growth for leaders and teams. How can you provide this for your team? We are here to help if you would like simple, insightful data for your team.

**You need a leadership baseline to measure reality.** It is very tough, if not impossible, to improve something you can't measure. This is why we always find a baseline to measure before working with leaders and teams. This leadership baseline helps us to know where to focus. It also allows us to show a measurable return on time and financial investment for our clients as we work to improve that baseline over time.

**Choose simple and sustainable over theoretical and complicated.** Most leadership efforts are way too complicated and so difficult to implement. Why? Most executives love complicated things, but being complicated is a crucial ingredient for failure every time. We love having five areas of a high-performing team because it is simple. There are only five to measure! And we can work on one area at a time and get results. Why does our approach work? It is simple, data-driven, and sustainable. It also works for rapidly growing teams with multiple departments and groups of people in different locations.

**Simple wins every time.** We have a saying on our team: *Hit it with the simple stick.* If it is not simple, it will not scale. If you are reading or listening to this book, you likely want to grow your team, freedom, and influence. I promise you won't scale anything by being complicated or theoretical. And you definitely won't create margin and space for your life or team. Simple wins every time. Answer six simple questions on the Development Plan to get clear on your approach for developing your leadership and team. If you'd like help with a simple plan for your team, our contact info is in the back of this book.

**In the chapter to follow, you'll hear Ben discover the five qualities of high-performing teams.** You'll feel the tension as he strives to get more time with his family and less time in the weeds of his business. As you hear his story, I hope you will think about where you are today in your leadership and how you can apply what you are learning in your specific situation.

Go to taleof2leaders.com for the *Tale of Two Leaders* Development Plan.

# CHAPTER 8: 5 QUALITIES OF HIGH-PERFORMING TEAMS

*All we have to decide is what to do
with the time that is given us.*

\- Gandolph, The Fellowship of the Ring

## Ben

In Kansas City today. It has been a long few weeks. I miss my kids, but I'm seeing them a bit more lately. I was able to fly home for the holiday weekend and be with Claire and the kids. I even got to go to a soccer game this season for the first time, which felt amazing.

I got a call on a business deal from the state of Texas that is a bit outside our current tech focus. I'd love to pursue it more, but I am still spread way too thin. I realize my limitations and my tendencies to overcommit.

### Working Towards Freedom

Today's high-performance group coaching call was helpful, and I'm journaling my thoughts here in this notebook. We were all supposed to show up and share our main takeaways for the past month. Here were my main takeaways:

- I'm still not getting the time I need with Claire and the kids. I want more freedom for my family.

- I still feel called to grow and scale this company and reach more people, but I haven't been able to scale the people required to do it.

- My experience, hard work, and tech expertise were once the things that proved to be successful. Now, these skills and strengths seem to be the very things holding our company back.

- What got us here won't get us to the next level as we scale up.

- I need to learn how to effectively lead people now, which is a skill I haven't really worked on until recently.

- I seem to be the lid on our team and in our business. And the lid is under a LOT of pressure.

This week, Jack shared a story about leading his own companies. He talked about hitting a lid and overplaying his strengths. Things couldn't grow past him until he realized he was the lid. I connected so much with his story. I've been the lid for our company for quite some time now.

## High-Performing Teams

I've joined the high-performance coaching group and one on one calls. I'm starting to see small wins and payoff in my leadership and in my family too. And I've recently realized that there is low-hanging fruit with my team that I can improve on.

I've promoted a few people to new leadership roles and am slowly building a leadership team. We did a handful of one-hour workshops with my team over a video with Jack and his team. I expected the team to be resistant, but they seemed to be open and get something out of the time.

So I decided to take the next step in our work together. I wanted to take the group through some of the same leadership content I was going through.

I have decided to challenge my assumptions and allow data to have a seat at the table with our people. We have financial data, but I'm hoping that data on our people will help me know what direction to go with the team and their development and performance.

I'm finally taking responsibility for leading this team. We are following the plan Jack has in place to take them through a simple team assessment. Today, we are going through the results with our top leaders.

I now have eight so far on our new leadership team leading in different roles. There are two operational leaders, three sales leaders, a finance team leader, and two VPs. We are all trying to keep up. Keyword: trying.

## Virtual Leadership Bootcamp

We jumped on another video call, and Jack welcomed everyone to the call.

Our CFO, Jamie, chimed in, interrupting him. No surprise there. Jamie is also known as the CIO: Chief Interrupting

Officer.

"I've done so many things like this in my career," Jamie said. "To be honest, Jack, when Ben first brought you in, I was like, 'Oh boy, here we go again. Another consultant with a bunch of theoretical mumbo jumbo that makes zero practical sense.'

"Our recent sessions seemed very different, though," he said.

"I have noticed conversations happening on our team over the last few weeks that really were not happening before. People are starting to treat each other with more levels of empathy, compassion, and understanding."

"Communication is slowly beginning to improve. We are beginning to have a better understanding of one another, and there seems to be more grace in conversations. People understand there are different personalities on the team and they are taking things less personal than before," Jamie said.

You could see Jack was ecstatic to hear this, and I was too.

Jamie continued, "I've heard team members ask how family members are doing. That is a first for this team. I've even had one team member ask how they can help on a project that wasn't even their project. We still have a long way to go, but I am excited about this work we are doing together."

"It is straightforward, easy to understand, and the tools are practical and actionable. I've also been using the communication techniques with my kids at home. I'm embarrassed a bit to say, but I'm having more conversations with my daughter at home too. If what we do next as a team is anything like what I've experienced so far, I'm excited," he said.

This was a CFO speaking. CFO's don't use the word "excited."

There was hope.

"Great to hear," Jack said. "Jamie, I've done a lot of these exercises with teams. They have to add immediate value. I don't ever want to waste your valuable time. If you can put something practical into action in our first few calls, that is a win. I want you to have an immediate return on your time investment. And when you commit to the work of personal and team development over time, there will always be a payoff. So are you ready to see your high-performing team assessment and results?" He asked.

Everyone gave a thumbs up and nodded their heads on the screens. One leader was obviously eating chips and thought he was muted. Those were some crunchy chips.

I could tell a few were still quiet and not as enthusiastic as our CFO Jamie. Based on their body language, the VPs seemed very hesitant.

I'm learning that individual personalities have certain tendencies. One of the tendencies of these two leaders was to be skeptical of anything new.

They weren't "against" me or Jack. They just wanted to make sure we were using the time well. I understood. Most people in the business world have had mediocre or even bad experiences with consultants or speakers. I was one of them. A lot of talk, not much action.

This was different. There was speaking, combined with visual leadership tools that everyone could use. Instead of information transfer, there was a focus on individual transformation. Very practical action steps were given too, which was different from most speakers.

Jack shared his screen and showed the survey results from our assessment, based on Google's high-performing team study.

"Okay, team, there are five areas we measure as a team," he said. "The areas are from Google's Aristotle study on high-performing teams. The study lasted two years, spanning many continents. Google found their best performing teams score well in these five areas," Jack said.

Thank goodness, I thought. Simple is good.

Jack went on.

"I'm going to review the five areas with you and explain what they are and why they matter. Like Google, we have found the higher the scores, the more a team produces and the more engaged team members are in their work. Higher scores generally mean they like their work more and are more engaged. Lower scores aren't bad. They simply show areas of improvement and opportunity."

### 1. Communication

"The first quality of a high-performing team is communication. Does everyone on the team have the communication skills and habits that are healthy and effective? Teams that communicate well move faster. They get more done and have less drama too."

"We suck at this one," someone jeered. There were a few

very awkward laughs.

## 2. Relationships

"The second area of high-performing teams is relationships. Does everyone have the necessary trust and safety to both challenge and support their teammates? Teams that trust one another move quicker and perform better. Team members that trust their leader have more open conversations. They provide one another better information to help the team and the leader move forward. These teams build connections to help everyone go further than they could on their own," he said.

## 3. Alignment

"The third quality of high-performing teams is alignment. Does everyone on the team know the vision and values of the organization? Does everyone understand how they contribute to the vision, as well as expectations for their role?" He said.

"Teams with high alignment scores take care of resources and perform more efficiently, doing more with less."

## 4. Execution

"Who likes execution?" Jack asked.

There were a few whoops and hollers. This team was all about execution. Someone actually shouted, "Get 'er done!"

Jack went on. "The fourth quality of high-performing teams is execution. Execution means, does everyone maximize their potential each day? Do people work on the right things and help the team reach and exceed goals?

"Teams that execute on the right things win their markets and outperform competitors," he said.

Someone let out another holler. Obviously, this was a team that liked to execute. And last, capacity.

**5. Capacity**
"The fifth quality of high-performing teams is capacity. Capacity means, are you resourced appropriately with the skills, capital, and people to achieve your goals? Teams with a high capacity are ready to respond to future growth and opportunities," he said.

"Make sense? Any questions at this point?" Jack asked.

"Seems pretty straightforward," said Peter, our new V.P. "I bet we score high in execution."

Another whoop ensued.

"I bet you are right," Jack replied, "Let's see where your team scored."

Our High-Performing Teams Scores were:

Communication- **53%** of 100

Relationships - **56%** of 100

Alignment - **63%** of 100

Execution - **76%** of 100

Capacity - **59%** of 100

**Overall Team Score - 62% out of 100**

"Okay, team." Jack asked, "What are your thoughts as you see your team results? Anything surprising to you? Not surprising you?"

The comments were varied and very interesting. No one was surprised by the higher execution score, including me. This team liked to get things done.

One remarked that the highest score of 76% is a "C" in school and still seemed low.

"The low communication score of 53% doesn't surprise me at all," another said.

She smiled as if she had something more to say. Jack asked her what she meant.

"Well, I know the heart and intent of those on the team. But often, we are so busy doing and executing. We don't take time to slow down and communicate. Instead of proactive, we are reactive. We stay in constant response mode in our communication," she said.

**Discovering Blind Spots**

Some of the data was a close match to what I had described to Jack a few months before. We did have several eye-opening blind spots though. We scored highest in getting things done and putting points on the board. We are great at this as a team, but it is not sustainable. People are tired. Team members seem stuck in the weeds. Everyone is worn down. I mean, I've felt exhausted for months now. I don't think I can sustain the pace.

Here is another thing I discovered. Because of the communication exercise our team did with Jack, I was now more aware of our team's quieter personalities. I knew there were a few people in the group that had not spoken up yet.

I wanted to hear their perspective, but I now knew their unique personalities and tendencies based on our exercise: not valuing their opinions or thoughts.

"Heidi and Justin, I would love to hear your perspective on the team scores," I said.

Heidi spoke up. "Everyone is spot on. You can't argue with this data. The biggest impact I see is one to two years from now. We have a low capacity, not enough leaders to lead in the future. This is indicated by the 59% score in Capacity. Our sales teams are still very immature and underdeveloped. They don't know how to read people and are often landing unhealthy clients that aren't good for us in the long term. Many of them are not coming across as authentic in their sales conversations, costing us deals. The lower scores confirm that assumption," she said.

I was shocked. I never heard Heidi speak up and give a bold opinion in front of a group like this.

She continued, "Also, our operations and sales team are often in major conflict with one another. We scored 56% on relationships. That score doesn't surprise me."

"Drama and miscommunication may be negatively impacting two things. One, our productivity as a team, and two, the client experience. I know our customers can sense the conflict. Because we are constantly updating our technology products, customers get passed around to different teams. If I am honest, I am uncertain we are positioned for future growth because of these issues," Heidi said.

Justin spoke up next. "Most of us are maxed out with our

time and energy, but I see potential in this group. If I could wave a magic wand, we would have a game plan for growing our future capacity. We've tried many things in the past to do this, speakers, conferences, and books."

"Usually, people leave motivated, but there is no plan for follow-up. There are no visual tools like the ones we are using here. Our team is too busy to come up with content or a game plan. We need to be out producing. So after each leadership attempt, we slip right back into our old ways, putting out fires and managing conflict between teams. This lack of follow-through may be why we scored a 59% on Capacity," Justin said.

## Compliance vs. Ownership

Our CFO Jamie chimed in too. "Jack, at a 62% total team score, does this mean that we are functioning at 62% of our potential?"

Jamie loves the numbers.

"Yes," Jack said. "That is what your team is saying. They are saying the team is performing at around 62% of their potential. This is not a slam at all on the team, but generally speaking, a team that scores a 62% has team members that are less engaged than they could be. They will do what is asked but generally won't go above and beyond."

"You may get compliance, but likely not a real sense of ownership and passion in their work. This is a general statement for sure, but we have found this to be true with other clients. The good news is this; now you have actual hard data to show you where you are strong and where you need to grow as a team and as an organization," he said.

My wheels were spinning, and I was doing the math in my head. I could tell Jamie was doing the same. He is always doing math in his head.

"This is likely costing us millions of dollars in low engagement and lost opportunities!" Jamie shouted out.

I thought the same.

"Well, yeah, it is a million-dollar problem most teams don't realize they have," Jack said. "Scores across the board are going down too with a lot of teams working in a stressful, remote work or hybrid office environment. Team members are isolated even more now, and problems don't get better on their own," he said.

"Let me ask you an important question," Jack said. "What if we could take your organization from a team performance of 62% up to 92% or more? What if instead of mistrust and dodging around answers, people trusted each other and gave the benefit of the doubt? How much do you think productivity would go up?

"62% is not a great score," one team member said. "Productivity would go up a lot."

"Okay. So what if, instead of confusion or misalignment, people bought into your plans? What if people showed up every day ready to bring their best in their work? What if honest conversations were the norm and no one had to question motives or decode emails?" Jack asked.

"People would never want to leave our team," Heidi said.

"Yeah, we would be the go-to place to work in the Midwest for the tech space. We wouldn't lose talent to our competitors. Tech labor is so competitive!" Another said.

"We wouldn't have to deal with so much stinking drama or gossip too," Justin said.

"Well, I would not have to keep bringing in podcasts and a different speaker every other month to motivate our teams. I don't have the time for it," another leader said.

I chimed in, "It would take a lot of pressure off of us, Jack. We can't sustain 70-80 hour work weeks. I've sensed this for quite a while now. The data says we can be much more efficient as an organization. It says we have a big opportunity for growth."

"If we went from 62% to 92% as a team, we would get more done in a shorter amount of time. The improvement would be a huge win for us. And knowing that people were healthier in their work and personal lives would mean the world to me. I care about our people and want what is best for them," I said.

Everyone agreed that communication would be the best place to start of the five areas of high-performing teams. We would work to improve scores in the five areas, beginning with communication.

"If Ben and I have a plan to work on these areas once or twice a month as a team for sixty minutes or so, is everyone willing to jump in?" Jack asked. "You won't have to come up with any content. I'll bring proven and tested visual tools and common language each month to introduce to the team.

"You'll get small wins immediately as a team. But, I know it takes 12-24 months of consistent work to see a significant change in an organization. I know this is what works based on our experience. We'll do a short team exercise once or twice a month on a video call. You can join on your lunch break unless you are a West coaster, but those guys sleep in any way."

A leader from the West coast chimed in, "Yeah, but we work harder and longer than anyone else to make up for it."

A few snickers ensued.

**Virtual speaking with 80+ tools and resources**

Jack went on, "In contrast to most speakers, you'll walk away each month with simple, visual tools that you can apply immediately as a team. You will become more self-aware and more healthy in your life and leadership. These tools and the time together will make you better and elevate your team to new performance levels. And we will be able to measure success over time through our high-performing team assessments."

The people who were unsure before were starting to look more confident. Several had already sent me positive text messages.

"I'll give you access to short five to ten-minute videos to watch between sessions. These will reinforce what we are learning on the virtual speaking and video calls. I'll even be available with virtual office hours for your team. You can book a video call any time by using our online link. If you need specific coaching along the way, I'll be available to help the team as needed."

"Now, you all agreed there would be massive value here.

I'll get with Ben on budget, but I am sure our pricing will be both valuable and fair. The biggest ask is that you consider going on a leadership journey together as a team. There are no shortcuts everyone. There will be months you don't feel like showing up or investing the time. It is not complicated. But at times, it will require your effort and commitment to grow as a team," Jack said.

I appreciated his blunt honesty.

"You'll have to continue to grow and adapt. You may even need to let go of old paradigms and beliefs. But on the other side, there is something special that can happen if you put in the work. Our process only works if you buy into it as a group and commit to growing together as a team. It works if you want to grow this company and invest in the people that work here," he said.

"We need to do this," I said. "Is everyone in?"

"Yes, for sure," someone chimed in.

"We have needed this for a long time now," another said.

"As long as there are no trust falls or walking on hot coals," someone else said.

"Great," Jack said. "I'll see you on the next call and loop in with Ben on details."

## Summary

**Based on our research, 82% of employees feel misunderstood, undervalued, and unheard.** Think about that. Four out of five people in the workplace don't believe they have a voice. No wonder so many lack hope and meaning. Consequently, leaders like Ben rarely, if ever, hear the truth from their teams. This data lines up with all my conversations with frustrated workers for the last two decades. This is why you hear the phrase "rat race." In the end, everyone feels like a rat. The lower scores on Ben's team indicated many areas for improvement.

**After surveying many teams, like Ben's, we have seen that most teams function at 58% of their potential on average.** We have also found the following to be true:


❑ Instead of high engagement, most teams deal with constant drama and gossip.
❑ Instead of trust and safety, hostility and distrust are the norms.
❑ Instead of reaching common goals, most leaders deal with misalignment and confusion.
❑ Instead of consistent wins, many teams miss targets and financial goals.
❑ Instead of maximizing team potential, missed opportunities are the norm.

**There is a better way! Imagine taking your team from a 58% performance level to 92% or more.** Imagine how much more people would get done, especially if some are working remotely. Think how much people would love their work if they were 92% or more bought in, instead of 58%.

**These are the types of outcomes we are helping clients to achieve:**

❑  A more engaged team with a healthier workplace culture, measured by each team, using real data.

❑  Higher levels of trust, with increased collaboration between people and teams.

❑  Common goals and teams working more efficiently.

❑  Focusing your team's work so they can all hit their targets.

❑  Maximizing potential and efficiently doing more with less.

❑  More growth in a remote or semi-remote work environment.

**I promise you, these types of deliverables will not happen by accident.** They will only happen with the right data, tools, people, and a plan to help you get there. I can tell you many real-life stories of clients who are building high-performing teams using our system and tools. Be sure to check out our Development Plan for a simple exercise for you and your team using the five qualities of high-performing teams. Our contact info is in the back of the book if you'd like to hear more.

**Let's hear next about Hannah and what she is learning** to grow her revenue and team. You'll hear her celebrate specific wins she is having in her life and with her teams. I hope her story will inspire you as you seek to grow your team, find more freedom and see a bigger impact in your life and work.

Go to taleof2leaders.com for the *Tale of Two Leaders* Development Plan.

# CHAPTER 9: BIGGER REVENUE, MORE GROWTH

*Don't tell them what you are going to do. That's vision. Do what you are going to do. That's culture. - John Maxwell.*

## Hannah

Journal: It is November already, and the leaves are starting to fall outside. The kids are ready for school to be out. The weather is changing, but there is one thing that remains as predictable as ever: Their dad is still being the world's biggest...let's say jerk.

At least he is consistent at something.

Nonetheless, I'm feeling a lot better this week personally. I have more to give the boys than I have in a long time. I felt like such a failure as a mom and still do sometimes.

But I'm growing and taking more and more ownership of my life, family, and business. I'm getting healthier in my relationships too.

Today feels good. And I almost forgot what good feels like.

### A Year of Intentional Leadership

I'm coming up on a full year of joining Jack's high-performance coaching group for leaders. I'm not always a huge group person, but it is fun to see and know leaders from different genres and backgrounds. I've also built a few unexpected friendships with other leaders. They are dealing with some of the same intense issues I am dealing with.

We all make one another better, and over the last twelve months, I've grown close to this little tribe of influencers. I'm getting results and winning more with our team at work too. It is funny; things are changing at home also. I'm less stressed, more aware of my actions, and more engaged with the boys. I'm not drinking as much. We even took a family weekend together recently, which the boys really needed and loved.

I jumped on our group call today. Jack opened us up.

*"You can't give what you don't possess,"* he said.

That resonated with me, especially after the last few years of feeling empty and depleted. I've had nothing to give.

"Hey everyone, we see each other on our video calls and interact a lot," he said. "I want to invite you to our place in Carlton Landing, which is a small town on Lake Eufaula in Oklahoma designed after Seaside, Florida. We have a lake house there and have rented a few homes for a day."

"These calls have been great. But there is something powerful about bringing people together a few times a year to spend face to face time. We'll use this time to build relationships and to celebrate and share wins from this past year. We'll also stream the event live via video, but

I hope you can make it in person. We emailed the details out to you this morning.

"For today, what are one or two things you have learned from this tribe of leaders recently?" He asked next.

I spoke up. "For those that are a bit isolated in their specific sector or industry, it can feel like your issues are specific only to you.

"The challenge here is that these leaders are missing out on the experience of others. Most industry leaders work with the same types of leadership challenges and problems. While some technical nuances and situations may be specific to one industry, it can help to know leaders in other sectors. You want to be around leaders who are leading people and innovating. We must all adapt to the rapid technological changes in our world.

"I love this community because we have leaders from diverse backgrounds. We are all learning, growing, and challenging one another.

*I've found the insight from a group of leaders to be much deeper than one person could ever offer.*

"There is vast collective wisdom in the group. I love how we coach one another along the way and help get our problems solved."

I took a day to fly out to Carlton Landing to celebrate the year and look ahead to the future. It is a beautiful place. We all went out and sat around the fire pit on the first night to reflect on the year. We went around the group to hear what others were learning, what successes they were having.

I was up first. I had no problem talking, even though I don't always feel like I am winning in my work. I'm becoming more comfortable sharing both the wins and struggles along the way.

## Learning to Celebrate

"I would like to kick us off with Hannah," Jack said.

Everyone cheered. This was a little weird. I'm not used to anyone celebrating with me. Something about it filled me up though.

"We've been working with Hannah over the last year. Many of you have built relationships and even friendships. Some of you are newer to the group. Hannah has put in hard work this past year. She is a very committed leader," he said.

"Hannah, I would love to celebrate a few wins you guys are having as a company. Around a year ago, I remember an issue you had with an employee causing drama and chaos in your executive office. Your team was avoiding this individual.

"The team was affected, catering daily around this individual. Remote work made it even tougher. You were frustrated. Clients were being affected. The drama was one of many issues on the team.

"If you don't mind, please catch us up and let us know how she and the team are doing and what you have learned recently," he said.

## Leaders Define Culture

"Yes, absolutely," I said. "Basically, our sales team manager was driving everyone nuts. I was at my wit's end. The team was more than frustrated. I had at least one employee quit over the issue, one of our best sales leaders. She told me later; she just couldn't handle this leader, even working remotely.

"I learned through this group the following:

*Employees don't leave bad companies.*
*They leave bad leaders.*

"I saw this as a huge mistake in my personal leadership. It was my issue and my lack of leadership. Because we didn't deal with this issue and so many others, we were losing top talent to competitors.

"We brought you and your team in, Jack. You did one on one video coaching calls with our leadership team. You took us through the leadership assessments. We started our monthly team exercises. We focused on the first two areas of high-performing teams: communication and relationships. We've been doing our monthly team exercises around those topics. We've used weekly videos and an online leadership platform you and your team have provided. You've coached our top leaders. It is like having our own Chief People Officer.

"It has taken a ton of pressure off of me because I don't have to come up with the content. I know exactly where we are going, and you come in each month and guide us through it. And in between our sessions, our team can access the content 24-7 without going through you or me. It is super simple and scalable to our many locations.

"Our scores have gone up too. I had my doubts about how

these 'soft skill' exercises would impact our bottom line. But our financial margins have increased quite a bit.

"With this specific issue you mentioned, we had several very direct conversations with the team member. Jack and his team came in and provided coaching with each of us to help guide the conversation.

"We discovered that the individual had several unresolved family issues going on. These family issues were playing into work big time. She wasn't able to focus on her work but was slinging drama around on calls, in emails, and the office daily. Spewing may be a more accurate description.

"A year later, I'm thankful to say she is doing a lot better. We thought we were going to have to let her go. I had already invested more than five years into her leadership. I wanted to give her a chance to win, and she has come around. We will need to work through issues, but at least we are on a pathway now.

"She now has a more accurate picture of what it is like to be on the other side of herself. The tools you have provided have served as lenses and mirrors. These tools have helped her to see herself more accurately and make adjustments. She is more aware of her negative tendencies and behaviors and how those have negatively affected our team and our clients.

"And I allowed it. I remembered this truth from one of our sessions:

*Leaders define culture.*

"I allowed this behavior in our culture. And she and

others defined the culture with her team, which was toxic and negative. But the issues stemmed from my lack of leadership. Because of my behaviors and what I allowed on the team, we had a lot of problems."

Curtis, a large home building company owner, chimed in,

*"If you don't deal with the problem,*
*you become the problem."*

Everyone laughed because we say that all the time in our group.

I went on, "The visual development tools helped me to see the issue. Like a set of mirrors, they helped us to address the behaviors we didn't like. The visual tools did the heavy lifting for us. Instead of a personal attack, we could use the tools and language to point to the behaviors.

"You told us that people don't respond as well to finger-pointing and accusations. You gave us lenses and mirrors instead. When people discover themselves in the mirror, they take notice. They take ownership of their behaviors and tend to respond.

"Our team is all responding. We have all seen different ways that our behaviors were undermining our influence. Our team has a greater level of accountability with one another now, a level of understanding.

"We all have the leadership 'lenses' now. So we have a lot more grace for one another and tend to take things much less personal than before.

"Our team is communicating more effectively too. We are moving quicker. There are fewer qualifying conversations," I said.

"Hannah, can you tell us what you mean by qualifying conversations?" Jack said.

"Well, we move quicker. We don't have to 'sugarcoat' or qualify our conversations. We are more direct instead. People are giving one another the benefit of the doubt and using the communication tools. It is helping us move faster as a team," I said.

Jack responded, smiling. "I shared with several of you one of the biggest mistakes I used to make in working with other organizations. We would work with a few executive leaders and come up with a strategic plan. It was a great strategic plan. But the plan didn't involve the rest of the team. So we would take this plan back to the leaders, who already didn't trust each other. No one had much buy-in."

"So no one bought into the plan. This lack of ownership is one reason so many employees cringe when they hear the word consultant. It usually means someone forcing a complicated plan on a team. The team resents the leader and the plan from the very start.

"This top-down approach is like building a house on a sandy foundation. Even if you have a great blueprint or strategy, the efforts don't work. Instead of working with just a few, we have learned to start with the most critical keys to high-performing teams: communication and relationships with everyone on the team.

"We like to build a strong foundation by increasing trust first. We get everyone playing together by doing value-add, short-time, high-return team exercises. Then as trust and rapport grow, we'll jump into more.

"This approach is night and day from most traditional leadership approaches. Most try to put in place some complicated process or program that some scholar came up with. Or they will pass around a book each month that few will ever read. Neither approach usually works too well.

"So let's go back to Hannah. Hannah, tell me a bit about early on for you guys. I don't want this to sound like a personal shot, but you said you were firing a lot of people. Almost every single week, like a firing squad. Many in the group are experiencing turnover with their teams. I know your story will help them," Jack said.

"Tell us how things are going now on your team. What have you learned? How is that 'churn' today after working on this over the last year together?" Jack asked.

"Well, I can sure tell you what NOT to do," I said. "Yeah, it seemed like every Friday was firing squad day. People even got nervous when we scheduled a meeting on Fridays! Seriously, I felt like I was living in a real-life episode of *The Apprentice*. 'You're fired!'

"We had so many issues with employees. The reality looking back was this: They never had a chance to succeed to begin with."

"I mean, we never set employees up to win, which is sad, I know," I went on.

"We brought in some heavy hitters too! But there was a huge lack of trust in our team. It was, like Jack said, trying to build a new modern building on a shifting sand foundation. We experienced fractured relationships and a lack of clarity around roles.

*We never really set our new talent up for success.*

"That has been a big learning curve for us: helping new team members win early on. Having open and effective communication as they start and as they grow in their role has helped them win. We are just now beginning this process, but you have helped us see that we need to be intentional about their growth and have a game plan in place ahead of time," I said.

"What are you excited to improve next?" Jack asked.

"Clarity and alignment around roles. And continued clarity around our culture and who we are as a company. If we can do this in the coming year, we will continue to grow and sustain growth. We can avoid bringing the wrong people on the team, to begin with.

"Our monthly team exercises have been huge for our newer employees. From day one, they get to intentionally build relationships with other team members. They get to hear what others are learning. They get to see people work in their uniqueness and giftedness. They are also immediately invested in. Most have never experienced this in their careers.

"It used to take a year or more to get to know other people on the team (and many would get fired before then anyway). Now it only takes a few months for team members to build a few supportive relationships on the team. They are doing short team exercises together right from the moment they join the team. A year ago, when we started this process, you were lucky to get time with anyone if you were a new employee!

"Today, we are hearing more from employees. Team members know themselves better and understand their teammates better. Turnover has gone down. We aren't firing hardly anyone right now, which feels fantastic.

"This is a huge blessing. We were throwing away hundreds of thousands of dollars on turnover, just like lighting a match to it. Hiring someone, having them work for a few months, then leave. Then repeat.

*Often, we hired the wrong people. Occasionally, we hired the right ones.*

"Our competitors enjoyed our efforts when that employee left out of frustration to join their cause.

"Our industry is highly technical in some ways. It can take a new employee six to twelve months for us to see a return on the investment. It takes a while for them to 'give back' to the organization and be productive. In that six to twelve months, one employee can cost $40,000 to $100,000 dollars. We had at least a dozen of those new team members not make it over the last year alone, which is so tough for both the company and for people transitioning off the team. The leadership process we have been on has helped us see how big of an issue this has been.

"We are now beginning work on the next two areas of high-performing teams: alignment and execution. The time we have been spending on communication and relationships has been well worth it. I'm proud of the team. There is a noticeable return on the investment," I said.

"Please tell us about the blow-ups, Hannah," Jack said. "I don't want this to sound bad, but there were several times at the beginning where you were blowing up on people. I remember watching you pretty much lose it in front of the entire team.

"How is that going, and what did you learn from that season? What can the group or anyone else hearing about your story learn?" He asked.

"Yes, this is a bit embarrassing, especially as a woman," I said.

"If you have seen the movie *Christmas Vacation* with Chevy Chase, there is a scene where the poor cat gets blown up in the carpet underneath the Christmas tree. Picture that happening on a regular basis, except with people on our team. After I blew up and went off on them, you would almost see a mark in the carpet of what was once an innocent human being, with a smell of burned flesh in the air.

"Thankfully, there are a lot fewer blow-ups today. Part of the 'aha' was gaining self-awareness.

> *I finally discovered what it was like to be on the other side of myself.*

"I've become much more self-aware today. I did not realize the negative impact I was having on the team. I was also stressed. I had no idea what would even set me off or trigger those blow-ups. They just happened, and every time I knew it wasn't good, but I couldn't stop it.

"I had no idea of one of the main sources for mistrust, drama, and a lack of communication on our team: me," I said.

I sat silent for a moment, thinking about what else I had

learned.

"I realized that every time I blew up on someone, I was shutting the entire team down. This created further mistrust and drama.

"Leaders define culture, right? And I had to own it. I'm still learning to own it. I was undermining my influence without even realizing it.

"I'm still learning now. Our team is learning now. Instead of waiting to bring up challenges or sweeping them under the rug, now we can address them in real-time. As a result, there is more trust today. I've done a lot of back-stepping to go back and repair some of the damage I was causing.

*Because of the leadership tools and the lenses that you have given us, now I understand myself better.*

"There is a lot more grace around the communication styles and personalities on our team.

"We have a long way to go. I'm not naive enough to think that we have the problems fixed, but we are making tremendous progress.

"The team seems committed to solving the issues together. And our scores in those areas have gone up too. We went from the mid-50s in communication and relationships to the mid-80s now, which is quite a jump in a year. And our other three scores went up from the 60s to the 80s too!

"I see a significant difference on the team. So, what is it going to look like in the 90s? That is what is exciting for me. We are going to continue in this journey. I also remember this truth from our conversations this past year:

*Leaders define culture, subleaders define subculture.*

"It is one thing for our leadership team scores to improve, but what about our middle management team? What about their interactions with front-line employees? I learned we actually have subcultures on our teams that make up our overall team culture.

"For example, our front-line employees at a specific location is a subculture. They are the ones that interact the most with our customers in that part of the country.

"We are rolling out the tools and training to the rest of our team this year. We now have the data to see how the individual teams and subcultures are doing in their performance. And we can respond uniquely to each team. I'm excited to see what the impact will be for the entire organization in the future." I said.

"Are there any other results you would like to share with the group or anyone hearing about your story?" Jack asked.

"Yes, for sure," I said. "Another positive result is the speed we are delivering projects to our customers. We manage some projects for clients. Our project time has gone from twelve to fifteen months down to nine. Think about that for a minute. We are moving that much quicker on our projects."

"If a million-dollar project is completed in twelve months, we barely break even as a company. There is a lot of overhead, salaries, benefits, equipment and contracting. We don't make anything on a twelve-month job. We lose our shirt at fifteen months.

"Flip that to nine months and speed the project up. Nine months makes us incredibly profitable.

"Our profit margin goes from nothing to about 15-20% or so, which is where it needs for us to grow and take care of our employees too. That is the difference improved communication makes.

"And because of better communication, we can hit that improved timeline on projects. It also helps when you aren't firing people every week," I said.

I stopped. Then laughed for a second or so to myself.

"Here is another exciting thing. People are in their roles for twice as long right now. The learning curve is much less. They can get things done more quickly. I'm not just excited about the scores going up. I'm excited about our bottom line increasing too," I said.

"Okay, let me explain something quickly," Jack said. "When we surveyed Hannah's team recently, we realized the people with customer-facing teams had much lower engagement scores than the executive teams. The executive team's scores seemed to be high with communication and relationships. Many had longer tenure and closer proximity. Most of that executive team works in the same city."

"But as you went out to the locations and front line employees, the trust and communication scores seemed to really break down. This was a big problem. These are the teams interacting the most with people outside our team," I explained.

"Can you talk to us about what you learned here, Hannah?" Jack asked.

"Sure. I'll say it one more time. Leaders define culture. Subleaders define subculture," I said.

"Yes, one thing we learned was that just because our leadership team felt good, when we looked at the data, several of our assumptions were way off.

"We had a lot of room for improvement. The rest of our team was too removed from our leaders. Because of that distance and the lack of tenure, there was quite a bit of mistrust. There were more significant gaps between the executive team, management team, and front-line employees than we thought. And a larger gap between our central support team and our locations.

"The central support team felt like their communication was more effective than it was. And the location teams often felt very misunderstood and undervalued, especially with remote work.

"We still have work to do, but the regular team exercises put these issues right in front of us. The high-performing leader coaching has been a game-changer too. We hear positive feedback from employees. They are feeling listened to and valued by their leaders. Again, we still have work to do, but things are looking up for sure.

"We have had the best year ever. Our profit margins are up. We weren't very profitable the year before, and this year that is going to change. I realize I contribute a fair amount of our success to this initiative. We've been successful by being intentional in our leadership and people development.

"You've told us many times the following:

> *All of us end up somewhere. Few of us*
> *end up somewhere on purpose.*

"We are being purposeful and intentional this year. Last year, we were accidental in our leadership and culture. Big difference.

"I'm excited about the team scores this past year. I look forward to moving from communication and relationships to alignment and execution in the coming year. People are eager to show up at work. They are sharing the tools. That is a huge win.

"I look forward to rolling out our program to the rest of the employees and seeing even more of an impact.

"Before, we were sharing books, and no one was reading the books. We would play podcasts, and they were all great. But podcasts and books alone are not a process. Most people wouldn't listen anyway because the topics were so random.

"We needed a specific process for developing the leadership and culture of our team.

"What we are doing now is so simple. The exercises are quick, short, backed by the right data, and all accessible online in video format. The value we are getting from this is significant, likely 10-20 times the return on time and the financial investment. I can't wait to see what is next," I said.

We went around and let people ask questions.

A few others shared big wins. Jack bragged openly on me and several others. It felt good to be celebrated.

Jack and his friend Terry took us out on a sailboat that evening to celebrate. The Oklahoma winds made for quite a sail. I've always wanted to go sailing. Terry's collar was popped on his shirt, so I popped my collar up too.

I guess I was a real sailor now. Ha.

Who would have thought a group of random leaders from around the country would gather in the middle of Oklahoma. Everyone was celebrating one another and dreaming about growing and serving more people than ever before.

I can't believe I get to do this.

God, thank you for using someone like me.

# Summary

**People don't leave bad companies. People leave bad leaders.** I hope Hannah and Ben's stories inspire you. Depending on the data source, losing an employee costs between 1 and 2.5 times the employee's annual salary. Losing one $50,000 team member can cost over $100,000 per employee in lost time, training and replacement.

**With leaders like Hannah,** I've seen firsthand how difficult it can be to grow a team while experiencing high employee turnover. The best way to combat turnover is by intentionally investing in your team and helping people succeed and grow.

**Leaders define culture. If you don't define the culture, the culture will define you.** Culture is more than retreats, ping pong, and latte machines. As Hannah shared, a clear team culture will help do the heavy lifting for you and your team. Some say it is like have an extra executive team member.

**A healthy team culture will guide, direct and inspire people to bring their best every day,** especially with remote or partially remote teams. With strong cultural elements, tools and language, you will have an advantage over your competitors. Without a healthy workplace culture, your team or organization will struggle to attract, hire, and keep the right people.

**People don't respond as well to finger-pointing.** Unfortunately, finger-pointing is the norm on most teams. People do respond well to practical leadership tools resources that are relevant to them. They'll use tools to help them show up with more confidence and self-awareness in their work. Want to do your team a favor? Help them connect to simple, visual, and practical leadership tools to help them bring their best at work and in their life.

**My biggest mistake as a consultant.** Early on, we developed fantastic strategic plans, but they were "top-down" plans with executives. This top-down approach was good, but it wasn't enough. To bring lasting change to leaders and teams, we now involve everyone. Culture does trump strategy every time, and a great strategic plan is only as good as a team's culture. Whether your team is 10 or 10,000, if your strategy doesn't involve investing in people, you are selling your team short.

**Podcasts and books aren't enough. I know this is a book.** It is not enough, though. I see so many leaders throwing around a book of the month or the latest podcast to help their team grow. I'm a big reader and listen to a lot of podcasts. Readers are leaders and we should all be reading. Nonetheless, throwing a barrage of random leadership content at your team alone does not work. Focus first on building a simple, clear, and sustainable workplace culture. Introduce clear and consistent tools, language, and vision to your team over time. Then supplement with books and learning down the road.

**Check out the *Tale of Two Leaders* Development Plan** to process what you are learning. We'll hear next from Ben as he seeks and finds freedom and passion again in his work. See where you connect with his story and where you can grow in your own personal leadership.

Go to taleof2leaders.com for the *Tale of Two Leaders* Development Plan.

# CHAPTER 10: SECRETS TO ATTRACTING, HIRING & KEEPING THE RIGHT PEOPLE

*Life moves pretty fast. If you don't stop and look around once in a while, you could miss it. - Ferris Bueller*

## Ben

December: On our first family ski trip in a long time in Taos, New Mexico. The powder is killer, and my back is sore! We went snow tubing down the mountain tonight as a family. Then we took a sleigh ride through the snow to a cabin, where they cook dinner on an open fire for our family. It was so beautiful and peaceful.

As the week is closing down, my mind is drifting back to the company and team. I can't believe I was even able to come on this trip. I've realized I have been the lid for our growth. We are trying to break into the tech market in Texas. But I haven't been able to get out of the weeds enough to work on those big potential clients there. So many companies are moving into Texas from California and elsewhere.

Thankfully, my team stepped up this week to allow me to get away. The calls have calmed down a bit, and I've jumped into emails at night when the kids are asleep. But I've been able to connect with Claire more this week than in a long time. I mean, how can you not enjoy yourself in the mountains?

I'm thinking about releasing more to the team this next month to create even more margin for myself and my kids. I can't pursue Texas and other big player markets without releasing more to the team.

I realize we don't have the leadership horsepower right now to scale the way we want. I know the process we are in will raise up internal leaders, but we need to get more of the right people on the team.

## Greater Freedom

"Hey Ben, what would a win look like for you today?" Jack asked. We were on our 1/1 coaching call.

"Well, my mind is completely renewed right now," I said.

"Yeah, I want to hear about those mountains!" Jack said.

I shared a few pics.

"Thanks for pushing me to take a family vacation. I've had a lot of time to think over the last week. My head is clearing up. I am getting out of the weeds for the first time in a long time. Being away was a good test of my leadership. The team really stepped up while I was trying to unplug," I said.

"For today, I'd like to talk about what you've learned about people development and getting the right people. Jack,

I'm really happy with the work we have done with the team so far, and I'm ready for more," I said.

"Yeah, thanks for the referrals and recommendations you are sending, by the way!" Jack said.

"For sure. Yeah, I have a question for you." I said.

"We started our coaching work on getting me healthy in my own life and leadership. I feel like a different person in some ways. My family and I have grown so much, and I'm so thankful.

"Then starting with the team, we've been working on our communication, culture, and team performance. I've thought a lot this past week about my family's future and our company's future. The mountains will do that to you. I want to ask you some questions from your experience.

"What is the most critical thing in your mind for us next, Jack? Like focus-wise, what do you think our top focus should be in the coming year? As I mentioned, we've been growing team health, culture, and team performance. What should be next?" I asked.

"Well, let me tell you what I used to think," Jack said.

"I used to think that culture is the most important thing a leader could build. I mean, culture does eat strategy for breakfast, according to Peter Drucker," he said.

"Here is the problem, though." He paused.

*"You can have the right culture and the wrong people. Now I believe that the right people are most important, with a close second to the right culture."*

"Think about that for a minute," he said.

I jotted down a few thoughts. This was really close to what I had been thinking about.

"What are your thoughts on what direction to go next? Do you think you need to focus next on the right culture or the right people for the culture?" Jack asked.

"Well, here is what I know," I said. "Our team is more healthy right now than it has even been. Trust is up, along with communication. I know a lot of that comes from me and filters down to the team.

"I know productivity is up, and drama is down. Fact.

"Also, fewer blow-ups are happening. I know we want to keep developing as a team, to work on alignment and execution. But I like where you are going with the people aspect. I wrote that recently in my journal. We need more of the right people." I said.

"Here is the thing," Jack said. "Imagine bringing home a shiny new leather couch, one of the kinds you see in a magazine. Now imagine bringing that couch into your home while it is in the middle of a renovation.

"Picture it: chaos, jackhammers, dust, contractors, guys using the bathroom in your wife's toilet even though she told them not to use it! And you put that nice shiny, leather couch in the middle of the living room amidst all that chaos and construction. What is going to happen to the couch, Ben?" He asked.

"Um, it is going to get destroyed!" I said.

"Exactly," Jack said. "In the same way, not too long ago, things were chaos in your world. They still are to some degree. Anyone you brought into your team would be thrown right in the middle of that chaos. If a new member or leader, a.k.a., your new leather couch, was thrown in the mix, it would be destroyed in a few weeks!"

"Now your team is growing and moving towards health in the five areas of high-performing teams. You are in a place to intentionally begin attracting more of the right people. Think about it. Your culture is getting healthier. You now have more personal margin for yourself, your family, and growing your business.

"The house renovation, so to speak, is not quite complete. But it is so much cleaner and brighter and more welcoming than 12-18 months ago. Now you can start bringing in more furnishings, aka talent, to make your house even more complete.

"Let's keep working on developing the culture and team. But you are finally at a place where you can implement a game plan to attract, hire and lead more of the right people.

> *"Strong team culture and performance is a good thing. Attracting, hiring, and keeping the right people is everything!" Jack said.*

"Yeah, looking back, we had a lot of the wrong people," I said.

"Tell me more about that," Jack asked.

"Well, you remember the disruptive team members from last year that caused so many issues for the team?" Jack asked.

"Yes, I remember. I'll never forget!" I said. "I had literal nightmares about them."

"I don't think we would have hired those people if we could go back. I want to take things to the next level. I want to scale our team. But everything still seems to revolve around me to some degree. I don't think we are bringing in and raising up the right people," I said.

We wrapped up the conversation that day. I was getting settled back in from vacation. The following week, we started a game plan to create even more organizational clarity. This would help us attract, hire and keep the right people to fit the culture we were building.

It is hard to convey in words what we did next, but I'll break it down in steps for anyone reading or listening here.

In theory, you could go through this same process on your own. But I would recommend having someone credible like Jack take you through it. Sometimes it is tough to read the label from the inside of the bottle! Here are my notes from our conversations:

## 1. Understand and rank core values

We had no defined core values. By accident, we had attracted some leaders and talent. And by accident, we had quite a few team members fail. These leaders didn't have enough of the right values inside of them. They lacked the key ingredients that would lead to success on our team. Here is a brief definition of values from Jack and why they are so important.

*In short, values are what wake you up in the morning, what gets you out of bed.*

Jack calls these core values. Most values are inside you, or they aren't. Values are difficult to put inside of someone else. You can teach someone a skill or a task, but it is more difficult to teach them to care about something in their heart. There are also what Jack calls behavioral values, what the values look like at work. These are the "permission to play" values.

For practical purposes, we call them all "core values." But it is worth noting the difference between the two.

*Core values are more about what motivates you. Behavioral values are more about how one's actions play out at work.*

Many teams have a list of values in a dusty handbook that no one ever reads or talks about. The book makes the boss feel warm and fuzzy inside. But when you ask these teams about their values, people hesitate. They say generic and vague things like, "We care about the customer and create innovative solutions with integrity." No one knows what that means or cares!

Or their values are on a poster in a hallway with an iceberg photo that says, "Success is the 90% underwater that only the penguins can see." What? No one knows what that means. Maybe the penguin knows, but we sure don't.

## 2. Clarify and define the values, vision, and culture

It is tough to scale a healthy team and grow without articulating the critical ingredients for success. So we looked at the top performers on the team, what they all have in common. We did what Jack called a "values discovery" exercise. We even looked at people who did not make it or succeed, what they had or didn't have inside of them, or at work.

Most importantly, we looked inside ourselves as a leadership team. What was important to us? What were mere "aspirational" values, those we wish we had? And what were actual values, those we knew were crucial for our success?

It was quite fascinating to look back and discover the behavioral and core values that are key to our success. When you go through this process, you'll have a considerable amount of clarity. You'll get clear on what you are looking for in the right people and what you are looking to avoid in the wrong people.

### 3. The leadership team commits to the values

Next, the leadership team spent a session embracing the values and talking through them. We talked about which values were more natural to each of us and which ones we personally struggled to live out at work.

> *Make sure you and your leadership team*
> *are truly living out your values before*
> *asking anyone else to live them out.*

There is usually a gap between our intentions and actions as a leader. We want to close that gap. We wanted to make sure we all felt good about living these out to the best of our ability.

We committed as a team to growing in the values that came less natural to us. All of us picked a value to intentionally "grow in" for a season. We worked to close any gaps.

## 4. Create memorable "sticky statements" with the values

Next, we crafted what Jack called "sticky statements" around each value. If the language isn't memorable, people just won't talk about it (Evidence: The dusty handbook on the bottom drawer or the iceberg poster).

We needed to come up with memorable sayings around each value that people would remember and talk about. These would communicate our values to current and future teammates and out to clients and the world.

Sticky statements are what Jack described as short, catchy phrases that people will remember and talk about. Here were a few of our values, along with sticky statements to help us live them out.

**Driven:** We deliver projects on time and under budget.

**Compassionate:** Our clients get our best when life is at its worst.

**Team player:** We accomplish the goal, no matter the role.

**Teachable:** We value growth over comfort and embrace change.

**Inclusive:** We respect differences and know they

make us stronger.

## 5. Cast vision and expectations around the values

Next, Jack helped us ensure people knew what was expected in their roles. Many were simply unclear. We communicated the values and statements and showed the team what these look like in everyday practice.

Over time, we re-enforced our vision and values as a team and gave clear wins and stories of team members who "get" what we are trying to do. I felt a huge amount of weight come off of my shoulders during this part of the process.

What I had intuitively felt and seen for years was now being clearly defined. Our leaders had a greater sense of ownership.

*Having clear values felt like having an extra executive leader on the team, a leader that would help us stay on track and know how to show up with work each day.*

Our team was spread out both geographically and physically. Having these values as a core part of our culture and the team exercises helped tie everyone together while we were physically apart.

Jack's next part of the process is one that some leaders are unwilling to do. It is one thing to have values identified, but another to have the courage and willpower to live those values out and integrate them into the culture.

Everyone desires a fair chance to live out the values in their work and close gaps between their intentions and actions. The tough step for leaders is to eventually move people off the team that may not align with the values in their everyday work. Most leaders are unwilling to do this, allowing toxic or unhealthy behaviors and actions to define the culture.

## 6. Re-align the team around the values

Next, we gave the entire team a clear chance over time to succeed and to know expectations, then re-align their work and actions around those values. This part was the toughest. We had to start having hard conversations with everyone that wasn't embracing the vision and living out the values. We held ourselves accountable, too.

This included tough conversations with a few key leaders. To value and respect everyone on the team, we gave every team member a chance to adapt and adjust to the values. Those who could not demonstrate these values over time either decided to go work elsewhere or were asked to move on.

For example, we had a very high performer that was not a team player and very divisive on the team. They did not really value being inclusive and respecting different people on the team. They were not teachable or humble in any way. After multiple conversations and plenty of opportunities to demonstrate our "team player" value, this individual was eventually asked to step off the team.

Jack says the following:

*If you aren't willing to say "no" to opportunities with talented people, you can't say something is a true value for your team.*

You'll know that a value is important to you and your team when you start passing on people who aren't a culture fit (To be very clear, we are talking about workplace culture, not ethnic or racial culture). Some people may have the competency for the role now. And chemistry will help them connect with the team.

But over time, Jack explained how cultural and value gaps will cause issues for them and your team. Besides, it isn't fair to bring someone into a team and ask them to be a part of something that does not align with who they are. And it isn't helpful to your team and culture to bring in new talent (or put up with existing talent) that doesn't align with who you are as a team. This lowers the bar for everyone, creating a culture of apathy and entitlement.

*Finding team members with the right values*
*is critical to your team's success.*

Many may have the skills and competency but lack the culture and chemistry needed to build a high-performing team over time.

## 7. Hiring and onboarding around the values

Next, Jack helped us create a plan to hire around the values. We started a simple interviewing, hiring, and onboarding plan that reinforced the values. The hiring plan was simple. The plan helped us avoid big mistakes that we used to make when bringing people onto the team. And it helped us to be more inclusive as a team to consider candidates with a wider base of experience levels.

Then, we implemented a simple onboarding process to help new team members win in their first 90 days.

New team members now received direct feedback and help growing early on in their new role. We gave all team members access to an online, on-demand learning platform that reinforced our values and was consistent across our multiple states and locations.

The platform measured and tracked their success. Each new team member was partnered up with key leaders. This ensured they had someone to talk through and process the tools and vision. This also reinforced our culture to more tenured team members.

## 8. Regular coaching for leaders

We then launched a simple process to have regular coaching conversations with team members. The process included regular performance conversations and annual reviews. Jack made the process simple and easy for us.

People are loving having access to the resources, tools, and mentors. No one wants to try to hit a moving target! Before this year, we didn't even have a target to hit outside of financial goals. Our unwritten motto should have been, "Wing it and bring it."

## 9. Quarterly goals, priorities, and execution

Next, we implemented quarterly priorities and goals for the team. The team has loved this so far. Everyone now knows what their priorities are. They are now able to devote time and energy to the important, not merely the urgent. These efforts have allowed us all to have more reasonable work hours too. I'm finally having more margin for my health, sanity, family, and for leading at a higher altitude. We are growing, hitting goals, and executing at a much quicker pace.

## 10. Monthly learning and development for the team

We invest an hour or two a month in team exercises via video. We grew scores in the last three areas of high-performing teams: alignment, execution, and capacity. Think of this as "drip irrigation" or maintenance for a team. Our monthly team exercises with Jack have been like a vitamin shot in the arm for our team each month. Unlike random books, podcasts, or random speakers, they are consistent, engaging, and applicable.

> *We reinforce our culture with practical and visual tools our team uses and remembers. The tools do the heavy lifting for us.*

This allows our team to do what it does best: bring cutting-edge technology products to help businesses change their world.

Jack has helped us create a leadership academy to coach our existing and up-and-coming leaders on the team. We are training up and developing high-capacity leaders. These internal leaders teach our tools, culture, and vision to the rest of the team. This approach is sustainable over a long period of time.

Jack will eventually step into more of a trusted advisor role. He will help us stay on track over the long term and add to what we have built so far. Our internal leaders will continue to grow and help us stay on track and perform over time.

# Summary

**If you want an engaging culture and high-performing team, you must have a clearly defined team culture.** Not a boring cliche saying on a wall, but active language and visual tools that your team will use every day. Without these elements, your team is nothing more than a group of individuals showing up to collect a paycheck. And a group of individuals leaves you with all the burdens you never wanted in the first place.

**Your organization will stand out like a light in a dark space** with a clear culture and attractive vision and values to guide you. You'll attract the best talent and people that want to be a part of something bigger than themselves. Here is a summary of the steps we took with Ben to grow his team and get results:


- ☐ Embrace and prioritize core values.
- ☐ Clarify and define the values, vision, and culture.
- ☐ Leadership team committed to the values.
- ☐ Create sticky statements on the values.
- ☐ Cast vision and expectations around the values.
- ☐ Re-align the team around the values.
- ☐ Hire and onboard around the values.
- ☐ Regular coaching and vision for leaders.
- ☐ Quarterly priorities and execution.
- ☐ Monthly learning and development for the team.

**You can have the right culture but the wrong people.** It takes time to get both. Most leaders aren't willing to do the hard work to consistently attract and keep the right people. Leaders placing a priority on people will reap the benefits for years to come.

**If you want more margin in your life, you have to give up control.** You can have time freedom, and you can have control. You can't have both.

**Releasing authority to other leaders isn't abdicating leadership.** It is good leadership. It is possible to find, hire and release high-quality people and expand your team's impact. Releasing leaders will take you further than you could ever go on your own. Finding and releasing leaders will not happen without a clear game plan.

**Strong team culture and high performance is a good thing. Attracting, hiring, and keeping the right people is everything.** The clearer your values and culture, the more you and your team will attract top talent. People leave bad leaders, but they also join great leaders.

**Being an attractive leader that people want to follow doesn't happen by accident.** The more intentional and consistent you are in your leadership, the more attractive you'll become to top talent. The more you surround yourself with the right people, the more impact you will have in the world. Use the Development Plan to score your team culture in ten different areas. If you need help along the way, our contact info is at the end of this book.

**Next, we'll hear about what Hannah and her team have put into place** to add value to those they work with every day. My hope is that her story will inspire you in your unique situation and help you to have an even bigger impact in the world.

Go to taleof2leaders.com for the *Tale of Two Leaders* Development Plan.

# CHAPTER 11: THE KEYS TO B.I.G. IMPACT

*The meaning of life is to find your gift. The purpose of life is to give it away. - Pablo Picasso*

## Hannah

Hannah: It was time again for our next leader summit. We met up on a video call this time to celebrate with the other leaders in the group. I looked forward to getting together in person again with these world changers!

We were approaching two years of work together and beginning to see significant wins and momentum. One of the last areas of high-performing teams is capacity.

We asked ourselves this question as a team: Do we have the right skills, capital, and people to reach our goals? Are we positioned for the future with the right leaders and ready to respond to any number of opportunities for growth and impact?

"Talk to us about your increase in capacity, Hannah. You guys have made a big investment in your team, your culture and your leaders. What are the main areas you have seen impacted with an increase in your team's capacity?" Jack asked.

I thought about his question and jotted a few notes.

"I would say three main areas."

## 1. Personal leadership capacity and health

"By that, I mean margin. We have more capacity in three main areas: on our leadership team, more capacity for our employees, and more capacity to impact the world." I said.

"Great, can you take us through all three areas?" He asked.

"Yes, for sure. I knew you would ask that next." I smiled.

"Personal capacity and health. When we first started working together, one of my quick goals was to get healthy and have more time for myself and my kids.

"I'm personally doing much better in that area now. I really believe the following:

*You can't give what you don't possess. Because of the margin I have found again in my life, I have a renewed sense of purpose, joy, and freedom.*

"When we started this process, one of my other goals was to create more time for business ideas and other product lines. This past year with the team, we've empowered three new operations leaders and promoted five team members to new VP roles. Before, I was spending two to three days of my week every week stuck in the details of our operations.

"Now I meet for about half a day a week with this team.

The result is at least an extra two days per week of margin for me," I said. "That's like 30-40% more margin."

"Has that been tough for you, Hannah?" Another leader asked.

"It was very tough at first. I felt lazy for sure. But it has forced me to delegate and empower these leaders with clear outcomes and wins. They all have metrics they are working toward, which they helped to shape.

"Now I get to spend more time mentoring and coaching them. I keep us out of the ditches and on the highway. Now I can maintain focus on moving in the right direction each month with our business as a whole.

*I've been using the extra time to get healthy, invest in my family and spend time on new product lines.*

"We've been working on a few new partnerships, which have opened up new revenue lines. These opportunities help diversify our risk from our primary revenue sources.

"Because we have more people in their sweet spot, we've also been able to refine our processes and improve our profit margins, a win-win for everyone," I said.

"Also, we are going to the beach this summer for the first time since I was a kid. I'm pretty pumped about that."

## 2. More capacity for new leaders

"The second area of capacity that has gone up is the capacity for new leaders. Our people now use and share the leadership tools you have provided. We combined the assessments, the visual tools, and the guiding values. We now have a simple process and an easy way to guide our team and measure success.

"Leaders don't have to wonder where they stand. Because of the increased communication and high-trust relationships, leaders get better feedback. Their capacity has increased. Our high-capacity leaders feel like they have a pathway for growth. Before, I was the lid for them, which was not healthy!

"Now, I've stepped out of the way, and they have risen to fill the gaps. It has been a big win-win for our leaders. Our leaders have empowered their teams. More responsibility has been delegated. Decision-making has been pushed down.

"This is creating even more margin for them to work on higher priority projects. It also helps our team to stay healthy in their personal and professional lives, which is so important to me.

### 3. Capacity and wellbeing for employees

"The third area of increased capacity is with all of our employees. According to our scores,

> *Our employees feel more heard,*
> *valued, and understood.*

"There is regular feedback and communication around our core values. People are setting and meeting goals more often, and morale has increased.

"Most of our new leaders come from within our team now. And most new employees join our team because of recommendations from existing team members. This is crazy! I have people on LinkedIn and Instagram DM me more and more to come work for us! Most of them mention the vision and the culture they are hearing about from friends that work with us."

"Not too long ago, we had a huge revolving door. You remember, right Jack?" I said.

Jack just smiled.

"Now people are recommending us as an employer to their friends. And these are people who often share the same values and passions that we share.

"I mean, I know I am a bit biased to our company. But, who wouldn't want to work with us? Not only is there a clear growth path, but you now have access to mentors and coaching," I said.

"Tell them about the leadership school Hannah," Jack said.

## B.I.G. Leadership Academy

"Well, we are using the scalable resources and online learning you brought. We have created an internal leadership school for up-and-coming leaders. We named it the B.I.G. Leadership Academy. Anyone can go through the B.I.G. Leadership Academy if they meet specific performance metrics.

## B.I.G. Education

"Employees can have outside school paid for, which is a game-changer for the less educated ones. They now also have access to professional schooling and real-life mentoring. We have digital and physical leadership resources for the team.

"We even added Jack as an advisory team member. This gives our newer leaders access to him and his team of coaches. Employees have access to career coaching, life goals, personal and even spiritual development. I mean, who does that? I can tell you, few in our industry are doing this for their team members.

*Our team loves working here so much.*
*Employees would have to be crazy to leave.*
*We already see our turnover going down.*

"Our best employees are almost not recruitable by competitors. They believe in our vision and are passionate about our values. We do pay them well. But they would find it hard to go work somewhere else and access the personal and professional growth resources available to them here."

"Hannah, I love the B.I.G. Leadership Academy & B.I.G. Education. Can you explain B.I.G. Financial Assistance to them?" Jack said.

## B.I.G. Financial Assistance

"For sure. Our employees volunteer to have a small percentage of their salaries go into an employee financial assistance fund. When team members have a tough time paying bills or have a medical or family emergency, they can apply for relief through B.I.G Financial Assistance. For example, just last week, our team covered funeral costs and counseling for a family that lost a loved one."

"That sounds like a charity or a church or something," one leader replied.

"Well, it is better than most charity programs. A lot of charities just provide a handout, which can often do more harm than good," I said.

"We go a step further. We don't just offer financial assistance. We also provide coaching, mentoring, and even prayer support if someone wants it." I said.

"Love it, the last area of increased capacity is the B.I.G. Fund. You won't believe this one," Jack said.

"B.I.G., that sounds like hype," one leader said. "Why do you keep calling it B.I.G.? Please tell me it is not named after a hip-hop artist."

"Ha, it is real," I said.

"B.I.G. stands for Build, Invest, Grow. These are our top three values. We Build and Invest in people and projects. Our people Invest in themselves and in each other. They Invest our resources and Grow our revenue, which is B.I.G," I said.

Several in the group laughed and a few smiled on screen.

**The B.I.G. FUND**

"The B.I.G. Fund is where we donate half of our profits as an organization. It is an employee-managed fund. We give profits away to charities that our employees help to select.

"Our leadership team gives input, but employees get to select the charities. We regularly donate to the fund. The fund then distributes those profits at the right time to several of the local and global causes.

"The biggest surprise to me from the B.I.G. Fund was the response of our vendors. When they found out what we were doing with The B.I.G. Fund, it helped with negotiations, believe it or not. Vendors learned we were donating some of the proceeds to causes they also wanted to help. The vendors were very supportive.

"They were also less likely to beat us up as much on pricing. Because of the B.I.G. Fund, they can communicate similar passion and purpose to their employees and customers. This helps them build a stronger brand and more passionate employees.

"We still work for a win-win in our purchasing. But our vendors and suppliers are now supporting these causes and organizations by working with us.

"We supply clean water in places that don't have it. We build homes for those without access to housing. And we invest in several other causes our team is passionate about. I'm personally able to give significantly to our local church, which is very important to my family.

"The best part is that our revenue and profits have continued to grow like crazy! We are expecting another record year.

I answered a few more questions that day. Someone asked how my life was different today compared to a few years back.

"I am still working a lot, but much fewer hours than I was in the past. My mental, emotional and physical health is getting stronger, too.

*You really can't give what you don't have.*

"I had nothing to give a few years ago. Jack can tell you. I was toast. And our team felt it. They were all working as many hours as I was. Our work and families were all paying the price.

"Today, I am leading out of a much healthier place. I'm happier. I'm doing what I love with people that I love. My favorite thing is to see these younger leaders step up in their lives and roles. Before, they seemed to have more of an employee mentality. Today, they seem to embody more of an owner mentality.

"We have given them the direction, the resources, and the coaching they need to succeed. They are responding, too.

*My phone rings much less in the evening
and weekends because people know what
is expected of them during the week.*

"The team is much healthier in their communication skills, emotional and relational intelligence. Employees are starting to solve problems I don't even know exist. They are driving our culture deep into the organization and to our clients.

**Impacting Cities**

"One of the cities we are working with recently called me. You'll never believe what they asked me.

Everyone stood there looking at me, waiting. It felt strange to even think about what I would say next.

"Ok, cliffhanger? Tell us what they said, Hannah!" another leader asked.

"Well, they asked if they could meet with us to hear about our B.I.G. culture and initiatives. They were particularly interested in the B.I.G. Leadership Academy. Jack and I are doing a video call with them next week. This is a large city organization that has all the right motives. But they are well known for having a terrible workplace culture. They want to hear about what we have put in place with our leaders. And they asked how they could build their own leadership academy."

Jack, of course, offered to join in. They have worked with many cities and state organizations. I can't believe we have government organizations reaching out to us to learn about leadership, growth, and culture. It is truly humbling.

The time was up for the day, and the call was dismissed. I went to baseball practice with my son after that. We then had dinner with the boys and some family friends. I can't wait to see what happens next in my life.

There is no shortage of challenges and struggles. But I can't tell enough how wise it is to surround yourself with other successful people that want to grow and have an impact.

You don't have to be an expert at all. Most of us aren't. If you are reading or listening to my story, you don't have to make ten years of mistakes like I did. Please don't do that. Your life is too short. Your family is too important. Your calling in life is too B.I.G.

Pun intended.

Learn from others, and get a plan to find what you want in your life. Get a process for growing your team and the people around you. I promise it is a better way of doing things.

And don't settle for a small impact through your team or organization. Your calling is too important. You are given resources to share, not just consume. And don't forget to pour into those you love along the way.

## B.I.G. Beginnings

I connected soon with Jack to discuss our work and celebrate a few more life and work wins.

"Can I share something with you before we hang up?" I asked him.

"Yeah, for sure Hannah," he said.

"Hey, I didn't share this with the group because I wanted to show you first," I said.

On the screen, I shared a photo from a social media influencer in our part of the country.

It was a picture of one of our B.I.G. workplace initiatives called B.I.G. Beginnings. Our team partnered with a local non-profit that provides resources and mentoring for at-risk youth in our area.

It was an artistic photo of the most beautiful group of young kids, all from different backgrounds and ethnicities. They were all dressed up for a dance in clothes provided from B.I.G. Beginnings. Many of these vulnerable kids had been mentored by our team members through the non-profit mentoring program.

The photo was black and white, with the exception of one thing.

A bright red dress on one of the young ladies named Amelia.

There was a signed note at the bottom of the photo.

*"Hannah, thank you so much to you and your team for the beautiful red dress for my formal. It has been the toughest year ever at home, but you have made me feel so special and valuable on the inside and out. Please tell your team what a B.I.G. difference you have made in my life." - Amelia*

# Summary

**It is tough to give what you don't possess.** I know we have mentioned this many times in this book. But I love Hannah's story and the transformation she and her team have experienced. I hope her story is inspiring to you.

**Unhealthy leaders produce unhealthy followers.** This is the norm for most teams. But healthy leaders produce more healthy leaders. The ripple effect is real. Healthy leaders and teams outperform unhealthy leaders and teams every time. This is the way the world works.

**Most leaders have the capacity for more. You have the capacity for more**. You wouldn't be reading or listening to this book if you didn't believe that truth. Growing is fun. No one wants to work on a team where there are no opportunities for growth. But to grow the capacity of your leaders, you need a process.

**Without a clear process, your best intentions will be that: good intentions.** With a simple and clear process for growing your leadership and team, you will see people more engaged. Your team will be more passionate about their work and more productive over time. If you have a process that is working for you, great. If you don't have a game plan for growing your team (most leaders don't), we have a simple and proven process that has worked for years.

**Employee development initiatives take time and resources.** If you have a newer team or a smaller organization, please don't be discouraged. The types of initiatives Hannah and Ben described take a lot of time to develop.

You can't and likely shouldn't try to implement all they are doing. Still, it is never too early to begin thinking about the unique impact you want to have on the world.

**Start by leading yourself.** Then help meet the needs of those you lead. Help people succeed in their roles and have the right support and resources to win. If you want to have an impact in the world, start with yourself, your family, if you have one, and your team. The cost of developing your people may seem high. But in today's competitive job market, the cost of not developing your team is a price you can't afford to pay.

**Think digital and scalable.** In case you haven't noticed, we now live in the digital age. With remote work and dispersed teams becoming the new normal, it is more important than ever to develop your people. Can your efforts be multiplied to 10, 100, or 1000? Can your team have access to support when they need it, 24/7? Is it digital? How will you measure success? Take a moment to go through the Development Plan page that aligns with this chapter and note any potential action steps you can take today.

**Even if your team is a few people, it is never too soon to begin to raise up leaders and invest in others.** You will help others to reach their potential in this world, which is incredibly rewarding. These leaders will also help you grow your team, find more freedom in your life, and impact the world. In the end, you'll have the chance to positively impact their life too, the greatest reward of all.

Go to taleof2leaders.com for the *Tale of Two Leaders* Development Plan.

# CHAPTER 12: MORE FREEDOM FOR WHAT YOU LOVE THE MOST

*Real wealth is time with those you love the most.*

### Ben

Journal: It has been a busy but good week. Time for my coaching call today. Big news to share.

### Road Trips & Willie

"What are you up to this week, Ben?" Jack asked.

"You'd think I was joking if I told you," I said.

"Try me," he replied. "By the way, is that Willie Nelson I hear in the background?"

"Well, as we speak, we are on the road in Montana. Yes, Willie is on the radio. Claire is next to me driving something I thought she would never drive: our new luxury RV."

"What?" Jack said. "You guys are nuts. What in the world are you doing?"

"Well again, you aren't going to believe this, but we bought this RV and decided to head to the mountains. We pulled our kids out of private school, and I'm going to spend the next month on the road with them. We bought a ski pass for this season and will be skiing all the major resorts along the way, which is something we've talked about for a long, long time."

"Wow, that is a big deal," Jack said. "I am so happy for you!"

He was the first person other than my team that we told.

"Um, what about the business and your team, Ben?" Jack said.

"Well, I know we've talked about this a lot over the last few years," I said. "But I'm stepping into more of an advisory role for a while. I've done what you have challenged me to do. Yeah, I have empowered the leadership team to lead at a higher level and take on more responsibility."

"For the record, we never discussed buying an RV and leaving the state. That is what kidnappers or drug smugglers do! Are you sure those are your actual children?" Jack said.

"Ha. Yes. I know. Don't worry. We'll be back home next month," I said.

## Gaining Altitude

"I've split the operations of the company up into five key areas. I'm still going to be pretty involved with sales and the vision and the direction of the company. We're still on track to hit our growth goals for the year. And we have a few big government contracts coming up in Texas and New Mexico, something we have been working on for a while."

"I'm so proud of you, Ben," Jack said. "You have come so far. I know Claire and your kids will treasure the memories you guys will create over the next month."

I couldn't believe I was having this conversation. I have dreamed about this for so long, and we are finally at a place with the team where I can entrust them with more.

*I've built several businesses worth millions. Having more time and freedom is priceless.*

"Please feel free to say no, but will you still be able to jump on the group call in a bit?" Jack asked. "I would love to have you share more of your journey with the other leaders in our group."

"For sure," I said. "I was planning on joining up before unplugging completely."

## Giving Back

I joined up on our high-performing leaders group call a bit later and shared our update. We were starting to see mountains, so I was getting a bit distracted. We pulled over at a roadside restaurant so the kids could get out and stretch a bit.

Jack kicked us off. "Hey guys, I asked Ben to share a bit of his journey with you today. I wish I could take credit, but he has worked so hard over the last few years to get to where he is with his company today. He and his team have put in hard work and it is paying off."

"Ben, it is amazing to hear about your road trip and planned time away. I can speak for the group when I say that all of us are having serious FOMO (fear of missing out) right now for your skiing and a month-long road trip!"

Everyone laughed.

"Okay," Jack said, "This is going to be incredibly insightful for all of us today. We'll get you back to your family asap. Ben, please give us a quick update on your revenue and sales goals for the year. Where did you guys come in, and what are a few things that you attribute to the growth and success?"

"Well, let me start by saying that it has been a wild year for sure," I said. "We grew by another 30% this year and will come in over forty million in sales. If I could explain the 'why' behind the growth, I would boil it down to a few key things."

I paused for a moment.

**Investing in yourself**

"The most significant contributing factor is a focus on my health, leadership, and well-being. I realize that may sound odd to some of you, but I have been very intentional this year to invest in myself and my family.

"We can't give what we don't possess. This group of leaders has helped me become healthy and more effective. I've worked 20-30 hours a week less this year than I was working a few years ago. I mean, I'm on an RV road trip right now, for heaven's sake. I literally just bought a new pair of skis for this trip!

"Yes, I can say that the boundaries and tools we have gone through have changed my life and family. My heart is full today, guys. I'm not sure how else to say it. The restraints and discipline I have put on my schedule were initially tough. But, I believe this to be true:

*Restraint and discipline lead to innovation and empowerment on a team.*

"Love it. What other advice would you have for the group?" Jack asked.

**Investing in your people**

I thought about his question.

"I would say get clear on your culture. Figure out who you are, what you value, and why you truly exist. It has to be more than just making a profit.

"Make a great profit, sure! But don't stop there. Focus on getting the right people that fit the culture. You have to attract, develop, keep, and empower the right people.

"We have been intentionally developing our people over the last few years. For years, we were growing so quickly. We rarely developed the people we were hiring. We paid the price too.

"Now, we have a simple and sustainable process for developing our team."

*We say, 'Hit it with the simple stick.' We have to make things simple as leaders, or we won't sustain any initiative over time.*

"Every six months, we assess our individual teams around the five areas of high-performing teams. Then, we work on specific areas to raise our performance on individual teams and as a whole. There is no more guesswork. No more wasted time and energy. Jack and his team bring that all to the table for us and help develop our teams.

"Having a healthy and growing team culture is like having another executive on our team. What I mean by that is that the clear culture helps lead us in a consistent direction over time. "When making hiring decisions, we ask, 'What does our culture tell us to do?' Our vision and values inform these decisions. They also challenge us to live the values out daily and not get too comfortable as leaders.

"When a team member is struggling, we point back to the values, and we help them grow towards those values. Even front-line employees are now starting to hold one another more accountable for living out the values in their everyday work. This takes the pressure off of our leaders too.

"These are our client-facing team members leading themselves and impacting those around them. The impact on our customer service is measurable and noticeable," I said.

"Now our culture is super clear, and we've empowered the right leaders. I have elevated above the weeds for the first time in years. I still know what is going on. I'm still involved. But a lot of the heavy lifting is done by the cultural tools and processes we have in place. Our leaders are healthier, happier, and performing higher.

*Our people know we are for them, and they, in turn, have pride in our company and its goals.*

"As a huge bonus, I've been able to spend more time with my family and kids as well. I've also created time for other work passions, such as new lines and partnerships. Now I can invest my knowledge in our team and lead through them, which is very rewarding.

**Multiplying your leadership**

"Jack has helped us raise up internal champions of culture and leaders. We all use the resources he has given us, and we add to them from time to time with our favorite books or tools. He is available now as a trusted advisor and leads an emerging leader group for us. I highly recommend an emerging leader group.

"We take newer leaders and run them through our culture and leadership process. We've also involved some of our more experienced leaders as mentors. In the end, our goal is to build up strong team members that don't want to leave and go anywhere else.

"We even added Jack's service as a coach to anyone on our team. They have access to him and his team of coaches when they need help. He even guides them through personal, relational, or spiritual challenges that they may be dealing with. I can't tell you how valuable this is. He has equipped several others on our team to do the same, which adds another layer of support to our busy team when they need it the most.

"Everyone, I've got to run be with Claire and my kids. They've been talking about this for weeks, and it is starting to snow.

"I don't have all the answers, and I don't need to. I'll leave you with this advice:

*Keep it simple. And trust the process.*

Everyone laughed. I love that phrase.

I jumped off the call, and we were about to be back on the road in Montana. We would be skiing in a few days. On the road again, as Willie would say.

Claire reached out, squeezed my hand, and gave me a little wink and smile.

The kids were back in the RV with mugs and gifts from the gift shop.

"Did you find anything for yourself?" I asked her.

"Yeah," she said, smiling at me. "The one thing money can't buy."

"Yeah, what is that?" I asked.

"I got my husband back."

# Summary

**Ask yourself, "What do I really want in my life and leadership?"** Do you want to grow your team, your revenue, and your organization? Like Ben, start with yourself. Healthy things grow. If you are trending towards health in your personal life and leadership, you will be in a much better place to help grow your team. If you are running on fumes or in a dark place, you will not sustain any sense of growth in your leadership or team.

**Do you want more freedom and margin in your life or business?** What will you do to get there? All of us end up somewhere. Very few of us will end up somewhere on purpose. You won't find this freedom by accident. Finding margin comes through an intentional game plan over time. Margin only comes when we plan for it. True freedom comes with plans like the ones Ben, Hannah, and others have put into action.

**You won't be able to scale and grow by yourself.** You'll need to identify, hire, empower and keep the right people. These people will need to have the right skills, passions, and values to help you and your team go the distance. When you help people get what they want, they will help you get what you want. Give opportunities, and you will receive opportunities. Empower the right people, and you will be able to lead at a higher level and grow. In the end, everyone wins.

**Show me your calendar, and I'll show you your priorities.** If I looked at your calendar right now, what would it say is important to you? Your family? Your friends? Your team? Make sure your calendar reflects your priorities.

**Restraint drives innovation.** When you place restraints on your work life, you will realize you can get more done in less time. You'll also give others around you permission to have margin in their life. Over time, people will show up in their work more refreshed, more excited, and more empowered to bring their best every day.

**Do you want to have a more significant impact on the world?** Most of us do. Ben did as well as Hannah. Start with the people in front of you. What is your plan to bring support to those closest to you? Your impact will be limited without a plan. Your plan may change. It will change! You do still need a plan.

**Be intentional, not accidental.** I don't know about you, but my greatest fear in life (besides snakes and some clowns) is being remembered for the wrong things, for things that ultimately don't matter to me at all. I've buried quite a few people in my days. I don't mean to sound morbid or anything like that. But the saddest ones were when no one could think of anything good to say at the funeral. What a tragedy!

**Begin with the end in mind.** I want to get to the end of my days someday and be remembered for making people's lives better, starting with my family and going out from there. I want to be remembered for helping leaders like you grow in their life and leadership to reach your potential.

**How do you want to be remembered?** What do you want to be known for in the end? I love helping teams and organizations grow their revenue and their people. I dream about helping even more people like you have the freedom to uniquely live out your passions, freedom to spend time on the things and people you love the most, to make your unique mark on the world, and make it a brighter, more hopeful place to live and to work. I believe it is possible too.

**You will need an action plan** to help you clarify your vision and turn it into reality over time. I hope you are taking advantage of the Development Plan. The Development Plan page for this chapter will help you to begin with the end in mind. You'll define success for three key areas of your life and create a simple action plan for each area. Need further help? We'd love to walk through the leadership journey with you. It won't be easy, but I promise it will be worth it. My contact info is at the back of this book.

Go to <u>taleof2leaders.com</u> for the *Tale of Two Leaders* Development Plan.

# ACKNOWLEDGEMENTS

*If I have seen further than others, it is by standing on the shoulders of giants. - Isaac Newton*

I am sending a huge thank you to all of those who have contributed to this project. A big thanks to the book launch team, who has given feedback, shared with contacts, and helped reach as many people as possible. Thank you to Randy Allsbury, Brian Hill and Cedar Gate Publishing for your selfless support and insight along the way. Thank you to Jeremie Kubicek, Kevin Deshazo, Chris, Mike, Bronson, and other GiANT Partners and Consultants for your guidance.

Thank you Macy, Meg, Molly and Myla for your support along the way. You are my greatest treasures.

Thank you Philip, Greg, Rod, Dave, Rachel M, Jeff, Dillon, Cindy, Jason, Cameron, Denver, Jim, Craig, Bobby, Sam, Jerry, Kevin, Robert W., Trevor, Miles, Ryan, Robert D, Rodney, Amy, Chris, Trevor, Boe, Jeremy, Joy, Jill and so many others for trusting me with your lives and teams.

Thanks to Mackenzie Richardson for your insightful editing, help and patience! Thank you James Meehan for your insight. Grateful to Michael Lane for your artwork and graphic design and countless revisions.

Thank you, launch team...

A huge thank you to Kristi Gulikers, Kyle Willis, Keely Jones, Maci Hestwood, Toni Hendrick, Kent Winfield, Gigi Faulker, Jason O-Quinn, Katie Pickens, Heather Spencera, Jeremiah Storkson, Jody VanOstrand, Katy Carris, Michael Grady, Brad Shultz, Dave Johnson, Rachel McKenzie, James, Amanda Raggio, Melissa Vance, Gabe Cap, Hector Cervantes, Lora Renshaw, Regan Gradke, Liz Surles, Brian Baker, Alan George, Matt Ford, Richard Mulligan, Scott Lesser, Levi Wade, Joy Missildine, Ashton Owens, Wendy Hennig, Tracy Murrell, Raymond Moore, Chuck Mai, Craig Boyer, Jesi Conder, Corey A. Jones, Michael Daugherty, Briana Bullard, Chaney Stout, Sindy, Leslie Rasco, Janelle Shellem, Scott Bell, Kris Blair, Chris Ham, Carter Gabriel, Jenise Tanck, Amy Watkins, Roger Bombach, Derrick Henslee, Robin Boney, Jason Schumacher, Adrian Hummel, Phillip Goode, Michael Finch, Terra Myers, S. Prescott Harris II, Audi Day, Aaron de Leon, Gina Lowndes, Chrisann Goad, David Lambeth, Makanna McCarty, Adam Thomas, Skot Waldron, Mason Mattocks, Justin Beaver, Donnie Anderson, Stacey Hiles, Mary Ann Loomis, Greg Gackle, Henry Rose, Billy Dry, Lindsey Kirk, Corey Errett, Blake Peebles, Kyle Sullivan, Joe Kim, Carrie McCarty, Paula Ford, David Brown, Yemi Ogenbase, Caylon Haggard, Ashley Karimi, Jackie Slater, Malcolm Hafner, Josh Wilcox, Barbara Baldwin, Tara Yost, Tracy Yates, Jeff Cato, Kaylie Farrell, Aaron Lee, Terry Van Winkle, Emily Tate, Leslie Hugo, Stacy Hiles, Rebecca Peters, Jessica Rimmer, Steve Mozingo, Staci Shultz, Kristy McIntire, Stetson Wadley, David Shelton, Dennis Clark, Steve Cockram, Lory Bacio, Mike Hardie, Rohan Dredge, Teresa Diseker, Kevin Kirkwood, Kenny, Robinson, Steve Missildine, Leslie Hestwood, Michelle Ponder, and many others!

# ABOUT THE AUTHOR

## Chad Missildine

As a speaker, coach, and leadership consultant with GiANT, Chad works with some of the most talented leaders in real estate, commercial construction, manufacturing, financial, accounting, insurance, government, churches, non-profits and other industries.

As a sought-out keynote speaker and coach, Chad has presented around the U.S. in many in-person and virtual keynotes, workshops, and other speaking engagements. Chad has mentored and coached over 1,000 leaders in 50+ organizations across the country. His company provides data-driven, simple, and scalable leadership solutions and speaking for teams of any size in any location around the world. He also owns and runs a real estate development and investment company.

Chad calls Oklahoma City, Oklahoma, home with his wife Macy, three girls, Meg, Molly, and Myla.

Go to taleof2leaders.com for the Tale of Two Leaders Development Plan. To book Chad for your event or discuss your goals and needs, email chad@chadmissildine.com or go to his website at chadmissildine.com.

www.ingramcontent.com/pod-product-compliance
Lightning Source LLC
Chambersburg PA
CBHW070004180726
48002CB00019B/1925